Getting Started with Apple Watch SE

A BEGINNERS GUIDE TO APPLE WATCH SE AND WATCHOS 7

SCOTT LA COUNTE

RIDICULOUSLY
SIMPLE BOOKS

ANAHEIM, CALIFORNIA

www.RidiculouslySimpleBooks.com

Copyright © 2020 by Scott La Counte.

All rights reserved. No part of this publication may be reproduced, distributed or transmitted in any form or by any means, including photocopying, recording, or other electronic or mechanical methods, without the prior written permission of the publisher, except in the case of brief quotations embodied in critical reviews and certain other noncommercial uses permitted by copyright law.

Limited Liability / Disclaimer of Warranty. While best efforts have been used in preparing this book, the author and publishers make no representations or warranties of any kind and assume no liabilities of any kind with respect to accuracy or completeness of the content and specifically the author nor publisher shall be held liable or responsible to any person or entity with respect to any loss or incidental or consequential damages caused or alleged to have been caused, directly, or indirectly without limitations, by the information or programs contained herein. Furthermore, readers should be aware that the Internet sites listed in this work may have changed or disappeared. This work is sold with the understanding that the advice inside may not be suitable in every situation.

Trademarks. Where trademarks are used in this book this infers no endorsement or any affiliation with this book. Any trademarks (including, but not limiting to, screenshots) used in this book are solely used for editorial and educational purposes.

Table of Contents

Introduction 11
What's New In WatchOS 7 13
So Many Models! What's Right for Me?! 20
    What's the Big Difference? 22
    Why pay more for steel 23
Will the Apple Watch Do This… 25
    Things the Apple Watch won't do 26
    Apple Watch Without An iPhone Nearby 27
    Wi-Fi Without iPhone 28
    This and That 28
Okay, So How Do I Set This Thing UP? 30
    Setting Things Up 32
Enough With the Setup! Show Me How to Use This Thing! 39
    Power on, Wake, and Unlock 40
    Adjusting Text Size, Brightness, Sounds, and Haptics 43
    Charge the Apple Watch 45
    Battery Health 47
    Settings on the iPhone 50

Status Icons 51

Gestures and Shortcuts 55

Glances 58

Force Touch 60

Zooming 61

Turning off the Screen 61

Launching Siri 61

Locate your iPhone 62

Airplane Mode 62

Side Button 63

Last App 63

Apple Pay 64

Handoff Between the Apple Watch and iPhone 65

Arranging Icons 66
    Grid View 66
    List View 66
    Removing Apps 67
    Arranging Icons 68
    Switching App Views 68

Installing Apps on The Watch 69

SOS 71

Noise 71

Breathe 75

Compass 75

Let's Make Faces…Apple Watch Faces, That Is! .. 76

Watch Faces and What They Do 79

Activity Analog / Activity Digital 79
Artist 80
Stripes 80
Breathe 82
California 82
Memoji 83
Mickey Mouse 83
Toy story 84
Gradient 84
Meridian 85
Modular / Modular Compact 85
Motion 86
Numerals / Numerals Duo / Numerals Mono 87
Count Up 87
Simple 88
Solar / Solar Graph 88
Utility 89
GMT 89
X-Large 90
Explorer 90
Fire and Water / Vapor 91
Typograph 91
Infograph / Infograph Modular 92
Kaleidoscope 93
Liquid Metal 94
Pride / Pride Analog 94
Astronomy 95
Chronograph (Pro) 95
Color 96
Siri 96
Solar Dial 97
Timelapse 98
Photos 98

Editing a Watch Face 102
Sharing a Watch Face 104

6 | *Getting Started With Apple Watch SE*

Finding a Watch Face 105

Removing a Watch Face 105

Making Changes on Your iPhone 106

Show Me What This Watch Is Capable of...But Keep It Ridiculously Simple 116

Memoji 117
    Create a Memoji Watch Face 120
    Deleting a Memoji 121
    Using Memoji in a Message 121
    Using Memoji on the iPhone 123

Messages 124

Reading and Sending Email 127

Managing Mail 128
    Flag an Email 128
    Mark as Unread 128
    Delete an Email 129
    Selecting the Inboxes that Appear 129
    Customize Alerts 129
    Message List 129

Siri 130

Making Phone Calls 131

Calendar 132
    Adding Events 134
    Responding to Event Invites 135

Reminders 135

Map 136
    Directions 139

Photos 140
    Pick an Album 140
    Storage 140

Camera Viewfinder	141
Music	142
Stocks	143
Weather	143
Activity	144
Workout	147
Fitness+	150
Check Your Heart Rate	152
Cycle Tracking	153
Sleep Tracking	155
Set Alarms	160
Use a Timer	163
Use the Stopwatch	164
Audiobooks	165
Calculator	166
Handwashing	168
Remote Control	174
Remote Play iTunes	174
Remote for Apple TV	174
Walkie-Talkie	175
Family Setup	177
Schooltime	182
What Other Things Should I Know About the Apple Watch?	***185***
VoiceOver	186

8 | *Getting Started With Apple Watch SE*

Zoom **186**

Bold Text **187**

Handling **187**
    Removing the Bands 187
    Band Care 188

A Little More Advanced **188**
    Force Restarting the Apple Watch 188
    Resetting the Watch Settings 188
    Get Your Watch DNA 189
    Update Apple Watch Software 189

So Many Bands and Accessories, So Little Time. **190**

Watch Bands & Accessories **190**

Official Bands & Accessories **191**
    Solo Loop 191
    Braided Solo Loop 192
    Sport Band 192
    Classic Buckle 193
    Milanese Loop 194
    Modern Buckle 194
    Link Bracelet 195
    Leather Loop 196
    Apple Watch Magnetic Charging Cable 197

Apple Cares? **199**

Warranty **199**
    Covered 199
    Covered with Fees 200
    Ineligible for Service 200

AppleCare **201**

Apple Music **202**

Appendix: The Apps **224**

Apple Apps 224
Index 227
About the Author 230

Disclaimer: Please note, while every effort has been made to ensure accuracy, this book is not endorsed by Apple, Inc. and should be considered unofficial.

INTRODUCTION

Apple threw a curveball when it announced the latest watches. For the first time ever, it included an "SE" model that was more affordably priced.

You'd expect the Apple Watch SE to be a cheaper device that lacks all the key features of an Apple Watch, but that's surprisingly not true. The SE is actually nearly identical to the Apple Watch Series 6. It only lacks two or three features.

If you are looking to save a few dollars and don't mind missing out on a couple of things, then the Apple Watch SE is a fantastic watch.

If you have never used an Apple Watch, the UI can be a little frustrating at first. It looks nothing like the iPhone and iPad interface that you've grown to love. Even if you have used an Apple Watch before, there are a lot of new features packed into WatchOS that you may not even know about.

Whether you want to use the watch for yourself or use Family Setup to give the watch to a child, this guide will walk you through what you need to know.

This book covers the following topics:
- What's new in WatchOS 7.

- What's the difference between Apple Watch SE and Apple Watch Series 6?
- What the Apple Watch Series 6 can (and can't) do.
- WatchOS gestures.
- Using Apple Pay from your Apple Watch.
- Using Family Setup.
- Using the Handwashing app.
- Tracking sleep.
- Finding, installing, updating, and removing apps from your Apple Watch.
- Using different Apple Watch features (such as SOS, Breathe, compass).
- Using different Apple Watch apps (such as Calendar, Reminders, Music).
- Getting driving directions with the Apple Watch.
- Using Siri on the Apple Watch.
- Using your watch to help take photos.
- Changing and sharing watch faces.
- Sending/receiving messages, emails, and phone calls from your Apple Watch.
- Doing a workout with the Apple Watch SE.
- Watch accessories.
- And much more!

Are you ready to start enjoying your new Apple Watch? Then let's get started!

Note: this book is based on the book "The Ridiculously Simple Guide to Apple Watch Series 6."

[1]
What's New In WatchOS 7

This chapter will cover:
- New and updated features

WatchOS 7 is the latest operating system available for Apple Watch. Unlike previous WatchOS updates which were pushed to almost every previous generation watch, WatchOS is only available to the following Apple Watches:

- Apple Watch Series 3
- Apple Watch Series 4

- Apple Watch Series 5
- Apple Watch SE
- Apple Watch Series 6

It should also be noted that not all features are available on older models. So if you hear someone talking about a great new feature on their watch and you don't see it, then it's probably because you have an older watch.

If you aren't sure what model number you have, go to the Watch app on your iPhone, then tap General, and About. Here you will see the model number. It will look a little weird—like MU643211. Just copy and paste that into Google and it will tell you what the model number stands for.

In terms of the overall look of WatchOS 7, one of the biggest changes is what's called List View. On older WatchOSes, there was only one view called Grid View, which looked like the below image.

Some people probably love that view. It's the easiest way to see all of your apps. The problem is it's also tiny. Some people have trouble seeing it and others have trouble tapping on the right app and will frequently open the wrong one. If that sounds like you, then List View will help. List View puts all the apps in an alphabetical list that you can scroll through.

To switch from Grid View to List View (or vice versa), go to the Settings app; tap App Layout; and finally toggle to the view you want.

Apple has been putting a heavier emphasis on making the Apple Watch a device that doesn't rely on being connected to the iPhone. This is especially true with the addition of the App Store app. This actually isn't a new feature to WatchOS 7, but it is a newer feature. Previously, to install any app to the device, you would need to do it on your phone, which would then push the app to the watch. You are now able to download apps directly to your watch without your phone.

In terms of new features, the biggest ones you should be aware of are below:

- **Family Setup** - As the name suggests, Family Setup is to help children (and even adults) stay connected; the idea is to give people who don't own an iPhone the ability to use an Apple Watch. This is entirely new. Previously if you didn't have an iPhone, then it didn't make sense to own an Apple Watch. There is a catch: the person in charge of the setup does need to have an iPhone. Once it's set up, each person will have a unique phone number. If you are setting it up for kids, you can setup different rules—like approved contacts and apps. You can also add a Schooltime mode, which limits what the watch does during certain times of the day—which means your child won't be able to play games while they are supposed to be learning. You can also track when your child arrives and leaves different places.

- **Watch Faces** - Apple releases cool new watch faces every year. If you aren't familiar with the terminology, a watch face is what you see when you look at the watch to tell the time—think of it as your watch wallpaper. This year, Apple has released new faces, but what makes this year truly different is you can now create custom faces and even share faces with your friends. So you can create your very own watch face, and then share it with anyone else with an Apple Watch so they can have the same one. That also means you'll probably start seeing a lot of companies start offering custom faces that you can download for your watch. You can also find new faces on the App Store.
- **Fitness** - It's a big year for fitness and the Apple Watch. As has been the case with other updates, Apple is adding new workouts (Dance, Functional Strength Training, and Core Training); this year, however, Apple is really stepping it up a notch with the introduction of Fitness+. Fitness+ is a premium service (meaning you have to pay for it) that will give you access to video workouts (that change weekly) that sync right up with your watch; so you can see in real-time on the video how you are doing.

- **Sleep App** - Sleep tracking isn't entirely new to the Apple Watch; developers have been creating sleep tracking apps for some time. This year, however, Apple decided to introduce their very own sleep tracking app. When you sleep with your watch on, it tracks your sleep habits and starts creating a sleep schedule and routine for you. That means it will automatically go into Do Not Disturb mode when you go to bed, so no one wakes you up. It will also send you alerts for when it's time to go to bed and even has a Wind Down feature to help you launch bedtime shortcuts—like a meditation app to help you sleep.
- **Handwashing** - You probably never thought that you'd need an app to help you wash your hands, but alas, it is here. The Handwashing app automatically detects the sound of water and motion your hand is making, and it will recommend how to properly sanitize your hands. That means it will count down from 20 seconds and recommend you keep washing them if you stop too soon. If you are out of the house, it can even remind you as soon as you walk through the door when you get home to wash your hands.
- **Memoji App** - If you haven't used Memoji on your iPhone, you are missing out; it

basically lets you create an avatar of you; the new watch app lets you share that face in Messages and other apps.
- **Cycling** - The Maps app is becoming a bike rider's dream with a new mode that gives routes and directions just for cyclists. It will even tell you if part of your route requires you to get off your bike and go upstairs. You can also search for things along your route—so if you need to get from point A to point B, but want coffee on the way, then you can add a stop.
- **Siri** - Siri is nothing new on the Apple Watch. What's changed this year is it now does translations. There are ten languages built in. Just call up Siri and say, "How do you say X in Y [language]?" and Siri will transcribe it and give you the option to play it. If you are familiar with Siri shortcuts on the iPhone, then you'll probably love that you can now bring those shortcuts to your watch.
- **Hearing Health** - Apple added improvements to hearing earlier, but this year, it's even better. It will now give you weekly summaries showing when you've been around things too loud, and also reduce the volume of your headsets to levels recommended by the World Health Organization.

These features will be covered in greater scope later in this book, so don't worry if you don't quite understand them.

[2]
So Many Models! What's Right for Me?!

This chapter will cover:
- What's the difference between all the series of watches?
- Why pay more for steel?
- What's the right model for me?

The Apple Watch comes in several different Series. Every watch—from the original Apple Watch to the Series 6—are compatible with any previous generation band (*some* newer bands are only compatible with the SE and Series 6, however). So, if you have an original Apple Watch, you can still use that expensive band you may have picked up. You can also find third-party bands much cheaper on Amazon and other online retailers.

The Milanese Loop band from Apple, for example, retails for $149; the below example looks the same but is less than $20! The quality is not the same, but if you just want something that looks nice, then this could be a good option. I'll cover bands in greater detail at the end of this book.

Each version of the watch comes in two sizes: 38mm and 42mm on earlier models, and 40mm and 44mm for Series 4 to 6 (and SE). Each version also comes in aluminum, stainless steel, and titanium—titanium is the most expensive.

What's the Big Difference?

Apple is launching more watches than ever this year. On paper, the cheapest Apple Watch (Series 3) might be mighty tempting, but is it right for you?

Let's breakdown all the big differences on the watch.

First, let's go with the easy: do you want this watch for your child? Apple introduced a new Family Setup mode to help parents who want to give their children a way to communicate with them without a phone. It's a great feature…but you need to get a watch with cellular built into it. That's not an option on the Series 3.

What are the other differences? The Series 6 comes with several casings: aluminum, stainless steel, and titanium.

While bands are compatible with all watches, you may notice both the Series 6 and SE seem slightly bigger than the Series 3; that's because the screen on the 6 and SE is more edge-to-edge and bigger than the Series 3. The 6 and SE come in 44mm and 40mm; Series 3 comes in 42mm and 38mm; this may not seem like a lot, but on such a small display, it can make a difference.

Speaking of screens, the one on the Series 6 is always on; that's not the case on the SE or Series 3.

The big feature Apple introduced this year is Blood Oxygen detection. It's a pretty great feature for your health, but it's only on Series 6; ECG was introduced earlier and it is also exclusive to Series 6.

That's not to say the other watches don't help with health; all the watches have high heart rate detection and Emergency SOS (although fall detection is only on the Series 6 and SE).

The compass is another thing missing from Series 3.

Finally, in terms of actual power, Series 6 is the fastest, followed by SE, and Series 3. The Series 6 and SE both have the same wireless chip, which is faster than the wireless chip on the Series 3.

All the watches are water-resistant (up to 50m) and have the same battery life (up to 18 hours).

Which is right for you? Personally, I wouldn't recommend the Series 3. It's a great watch, but it was released several years ago, which means it won't be supported much longer. For $79 more, you can get a much more powerful watch with the SE. For the most optimal experience, then obviously Series 6 is the best choice—but the features aren't that much different than the SE, so you have to ask yourself if it's worth the price you'll pay for it.

Why Pay More for Steel

Which watch is right for you? If you have an itching to spend $1k+ for a watch, then you are probably considering the steel model with Hermes band over the sports model. What's the difference? In terms of wear and tear, both watches will hold up pretty well; every watch—even the more expensive ones—has the same hardware. The steel model has a stronger display that is slightly more scratch-resistant.

Unlike the iPhone or iPad, you aren't paying more for more memory—you are paying for the finish—so it's really a question of taste. The steel watch is slick, smooth and shiny. If you can afford it and want something a little classier, then the steel watch is a good option.

You might also consider skin allergies when picking the finish. Most people will have absolutely no problem with aluminum; my wife, however, has a sensitivity to it—her only option is stainless steel, which tends to be more hypoallergenic.

Also, if you already have the watch and don't like the band, you are able to return the band (even if it's opened) to any Apple Store within 14 days for a band of equal value. (Note: this offer will not necessarily run forever, so check with your local store before going in for an exchange.)

[3]
WILL THE APPLE WATCH DO THIS...

This chapter will cover:
- What the Apple Watch won't do
- What the Apple Watch will do without an iPhone nearby
- What the Apple Watch will do on Wi-Fi without an iPhone nearby
- This and that

When you think about the watch, you might have certain expectations—perhaps it's watching Netflix from your wrist or FaceTime with your friends. So before continuing to how the watch works, let me cover really quickly the major things the watch cannot do (that some people think it can)—and what it can do.

THINGS THE APPLE WATCH WON'T DO...

- Play videos; it can render very small clips, but don't plan on watching *The Lord of the Rings* on your wrist.
- Type messages; there is no onboard keyboard...just a microphone. You can scribble to type (we'll cover that later).
- Play games; while Apple Watch games do exist, the watch is a companion to the phone, and meant for viewing short messages...not playing games. So yes, you can play games, but this is not what you want to get to meet your gaming needs.
- Sync with non-Apple phones; the Apple Watch will not work with any phone but iPhone. Family Setup has added a very big *but* here. With Family Setup, you can use your iPhone to setup other watches, which means you can theoretically use it without an iPhone; that's great for kids and some adults. But if you are really into fitness, then you'll probably want the option to sync it with your phone, and if you are a non-iPhone user, that's not going to be possible.
- Work with older phones; the Apple Watch is for iPhone 5 and up.

- Work with traditional headphones; there's no audio input on the Apple Watch. It does work with Bluetooth headphones, but these are not included with the watch.
- Take a photo; you can view photos on the watch—you can even use it as an external viewfinder to take a photo on your iPhone—but the watch has no built-in camera.

APPLE WATCH WITHOUT AN IPHONE NEARBY

To be entirely clear, you must own an iPhone to use the Apple Watch (unless you are using Family Setup). The watch is not compatible with Android or any other smartphone. But you don't have to take your iPhone everywhere to use the watch. And if you have cellular on the watch, there's more you can do here without your phone nearby. Here are some of the things you can do if you don't have your phone nearby:

- Set the time.
- Play music (you can put up to 2 GB of songs on your watch…to put it another way, that's about 500 songs).
- Track your run / exercise—it will keep a record of things like calories burned, heart rate, and distance / pace, and then sync it to your phone when you have it nearby again.
- Track your standing time and steps.
- See your photos—75 MB is reserved for photos.

- Read, delete and flag email that has come in.
- Use the alarm, stopwatch, and timer.
- Use Passbook to show tickets (like an airplane or concert ticket).
- Use Apple Pay to buy things.

Wi-Fi Without iPhone

And here's what you can do if you don't have your phone, but you do have Wi-Fi:
- Send and receive text messages and use digital touch messages (i.e. drawing and tapping patterns to send as a message).
- Use Siri.

This and That

A few other things you might need to know about the watch…
- It takes about two hours to fully charge your Apple Watch.
- It takes your iPhone's battery…kind of; because the watch talks to your phone, your phone's battery will be used. It's not significant, but it's enough that you might notice 30 minutes to an hour of usage gone by the end of the day that used to be there.
- There's a feature on the device called "Taptic Engine"—fancy sounding, right? But what is it? The Taptic Engine lets you receive

feedback on your wrist that feels like someone is tapping you.
- You can use it as a phone...sort of. Yes, it sounds very Dick Tracy-like to get phone calls on your wrist, but don't get too excited—it's a little awkward to use; to get the most out of it, you really need to put it up to your mouth. And the audio that comes out of the speakers is subpar at best.
- It tells time! Well yes—you probably knew that. But it also tells time very precisely (within 50 milliseconds), which makes it one of the most accurate watches ever made.

[4]
Okay, So How Do I Set This Thing Up?

This chapter will cover:
- Setting up the Apple Watch for the first time
- Restoring from a previous generation Apple Watch

This chapter is all about taking it out of the box and setting it up for the first time. You might be perfectly comfortable doing this without reading how. If that's the case, then skip ahead to the next chapter—you won't miss anything here.

The process is pretty simple, but if you want an explanation of what it's actually doing in each step—like why it asks about privacy—then read on.

I'm not big on unboxings. You know what's in the box by looking at the box. But with the latest Apple Watch, there is something very important worth pointing out about the box. It's not what's inside it…it's what's *not* inside it. A charging adapter! A charger cable is, however, included.

In an effort to be more environmentally friendly, Apple has skipped boxing charger adapters with the device.

If you need to buy one, the official adapter is $19. You can buy non-official ones for cheaper, but as they are not endorsed by Apple, use at your own risk.

If you happen to be just updating your watch, then you can do it on the watch itself (you no longer have to do it on your iPhone as you did on the earlier watches); just go to the Settings app > General > Software Update.

NOTE TO USERS UPDATING: If you are updating your iPhone and watch from a previous OS, there's a chance you will have to reformat your watch to get it to sync. If that happens, then from your watch you need to go to Settings > General > Reset; next tap Erase All Content and Settings.

Getting Started With Apple Watch SE

Setting Things Up

Once you have the watch out of the box, push the side button to turn it on. You get the following screen:

Because the Apple Watch has no keyboards, setup is a bit unusual compared to other Apple products. Setup for the watch actually begins not with the watch, but with the iPhone.

If you aren't running iPhone iOS 12 and up, then the first thing you need to do is update your phone (ideally, you want iOS 14 on your iPhone). You also need at least an iPhone 5—anything less will not be compatible. To see if your phone needs to be updated, go to Settings on the iPhone, then General, and finally Software Update—it will tell you if your phone is up-to-date.

If you are up-to-date on everything, then go to the Watch app, and tap Start Pairing. This gives you the below setup screen.

Place your watch (make sure it's turned on) within that square box. You'll notice your watch has a moving image on its screen now. In just a few seconds, it will say your watch is paired.

From here you can either Restore from a backup or Set Up as a new watch. If you've never owned an Apple Watch (or you want to start fresh), then select the second choice. If you've owned previous generations, then select the first (this will put all your preferences from your old watch on your new watch). Assuming you are setting it up as a new watch, the next screen will ask if you are wearing the watch on your left or right wrist. Based on your answer, the orientation of the watch will change (you can change this later).

Next you'll need to agree to the terms. Feel free to read it thoroughly through—then give it to your lawyer to ask what they think...or just hit Agree like everyone else. After you agree to the terms, you'll get a message telling you some apps will use things like your location. That sounds scary, but what it basically means is if you want to use a map to get directions, then it has to know where you are first. Your only option here is to hit OK.

After you agree to share your location with apps, you need to add a passcode. This works much like your phone (before your phone had fingerprint to unlock or Face ID). You don't have to add a passcode. Adding it protects your watch from someone stealing it and then using it.

Is Apple breaking your heart with this setup? The next screen will help detect it! It tells you all about the new heart monitor feature. Read it and then hit Continue.

Next is SOS. This feature will text your contacts to tell them if you are in trouble. It's sort of like Apple's version of "I've fallen and I can't get up." Read it and hit Continue to proceed.

You may not have known it, but a lot of your favorite apps already have Watch apps. You can add everything that you already own, or pick and choose them later. Personally, I would be careful of selecting all of them. This is the easiest option, but you'll probably find a lot of your favorite phone apps are sort of pointless on your wrist.

You're just about done. Your phone and watch are now syncing with all the settings you just selected. If you decided to install all apps, it will take a few minutes to finish. Along the way you'll probably also get a message about your phone and watch now sharing text messages—that just means if someone texts you, you'll get it on your wrist too.

A message will now appear on both your phone and watch saying it's done. You can now use your watch!

[5]
ENOUGH WITH THE SETUP! SHOW ME HOW TO USE THIS THING!

This chapter will cover:
- Adjusting settings
- What status icons represent
- What happened to Force Touch?
- Gestures and shortcuts
- Arranging icons
- Handoff between Apple Watch and iPhone

Setup is pretty self-explanatory, right? What you *really* are waiting for is how to use this thing! So let's get started!

Power On, Wake, and Unlock

To turn your watch on, press and hold the side button until the Apple logo appears; to turn it off press and hold the side button until a slider appears telling you to drag it to the right to power off.

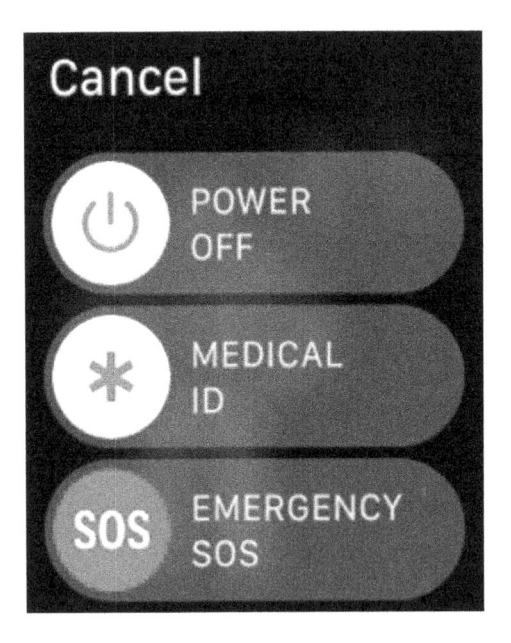

Taking your watch off standby is the most seamless thing you'll do—just lift your wrist! How's that for easy? Turning standby back on is just as simple—put your wrist down.

If you lift your wrist and standby doesn't turn off, then it's possible that you changed a setting. Open the Settings button on the Home screen of your watch (it looks just like the one on your phone except it's round), and then go to General and Orientation—make sure Orientation is set to the wrist that you wear—if you are wearing it on your right hand and Orientation is set to left hand, for example, then change it. The other thing that might have happened is your battery has drained.

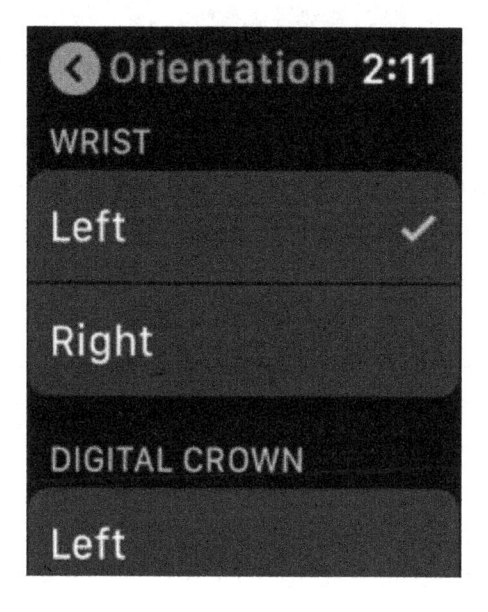

When you lift your wrist, the watch will either show your watch face (i.e. time) or the last app opened. By default, it shows the watch face, but if you want it to go to your last activity, then go to Settings, then General, and finally Wake Screen—once you tap this, pick Resume Previous Activity.

You also have the ability to unlock the watch with your phone using a passcode. This is a great feature if you take your watch off a lot. It doesn't mean you need to put in a passcode every time you look at the time—it only needs it when the watch is off your wrist or being worn too loosely. The passcode can be the same as the phone, but it's recommended that the code is different. To activate Passcode, go to Settings from your watch's Home screen, and then scroll down until you see Passcode, then tap it. Tap Turn on Unlock with iPhone. If you ever want to change it, just follow the same steps, but pick Change Passcode.

If you ever forget your passcode, then unpair your watch from the iPhone and erase all the settings.

Adjusting Text Size, Brightness, Sounds, and Haptics

I hope you love settings, because that's where we'll stay for this section!

The Apple Watch is probably smaller than you're used to when reading messages, emails, news, etc.; if it's too small then you can make text larger by going to Brightness and Text Size, tap Text Size and then use the Digital Crown knob to increase or decrease it. You can also check or uncheck making the text boldface. (Note: before boldface is in place, the watch will need to be reset.)

From this same menu, you can adjust how bright the watch is.

If you don't like the default sounds on your watch, then go to Sounds & Haptics from the Settings menu. Use your Digital Crown knob to adjust how loud it gets. You can also mute sounds by switching to Silent mode. (Note: muting does not turn off sound on alarms.)

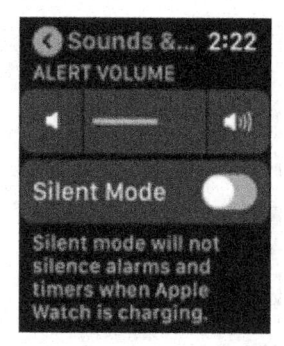

For some notifications, you will get a tap on your wrist, which you may love or hate. If you hate it, then go back to the previous menu. Next, go to the Haptic section and you can toggle it on or off—and also make it more prominent.

CHARGE THE APPLE WATCH

Charging your watch is very simple; it might be a little strange at first, because the charger is magnetic and doesn't plug into the watch—rather it snaps into the back. Make sure you use the charger that came with your device—using any other might overcharge the device, which will drain the battery quickly.

It takes about two hours to fully charge the watch.

If you want to know how much time is needed for a full charge, swipe up from the watch face, which brings up Glances, and then swipe to the Battery glance.

When the watch has less than 10% power left, it will automatically go into a Power Reserve mode—in this mode, the watch will show the time, but other apps won't be available. You can also manually turn Power Reserve on by pressing the side button for three seconds until the Power menu comes up, then swiping Power Reserve.

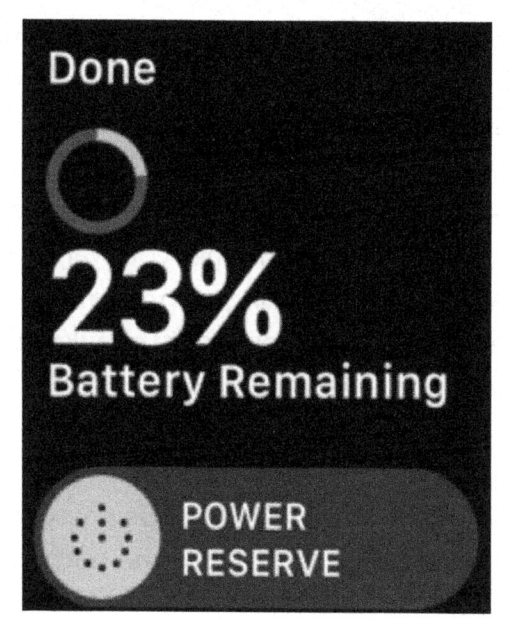

You can see how much time you have left in your battery reserve at any time by swiping up from the watch face to bring up Glances, then swiping to Power Reserve. You can also use the Apple Watch app on your iPhone to see the last time you charged it.

NOTE: Anytime I mention Glances in this book, that just means swipe up from your devices—there are a lot of Glances I'll be covering.

Battery Health

Battery life is important to any gadget, but this is especially true to the Apple Watch; you want to use it to track fitness goals and even track sleep—

for some people, you'll want to leave it on all the time. But you have to charge it at some point. Battery health options help you get the most out of your battery.

There are really two big problems when it comes to battery health: one, you want to make sure you can use it as long as possible before charging it; and two, you want to make sure it's not overcharging.

For example, if you leave your watch charging all night, then at some point in the night, it will be fully charged—but it will continue charging. That's going to add wear and tear to the battery inside. You can turn on Optimized Battery Charging to learn about your charging habits. If it notices you are mostly charging it through the night, then it will charge it to 80%, and then charge the remaining 20% an hour before you normally get up. This is going to keep the battery healthy for longer.

To get started, go into the Settings app, then tap Battery. This is going to show you an overview of your battery. In my case, the battery is at 61%.

If I scroll down (or turn the Digital Crown), there's an option to manually slide on Power Reserve mode, and above that, a button for Battery Health.

When you tap the Battery Health button, you'll see what your battery life is currently at. In the example below, the Maximum Capacity is 86%.

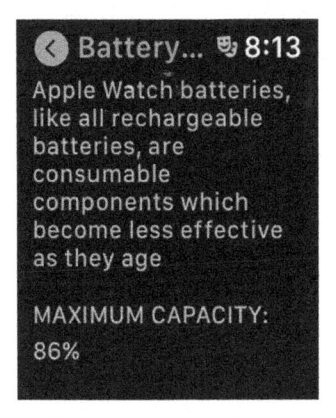

> **Battery... 8:13**
>
> Apple Watch batteries, like all rechargeable batteries, are consumable components which become less effective as they age
>
> MAXIMUM CAPACITY:
> 86%

Scroll down a little, and you'll see an option to toggle Optimized Battery Charging on and off.

> **Battery... 8:13**
>
> Optimized Battery Charging
>
> To reduce battery aging, Apple Watch learns from your daily charging routine so it can wait to finish charging past 80% until

Settings on the iPhone

Now that we covered all the settings, here's a hint you'll probably be annoyed I didn't tell you about earlier: you can do almost all of this on your iPhone!

You don't always have your phone on you, so you should know where they are on both the watch and the phone. Most people will find it easier to control settings on a larger device, however.

To adjust the settings, go to your Watch app on the phone, and then scroll down to the setting you want. Anything you change here will sync to your watch automatically. There's nothing else to do!

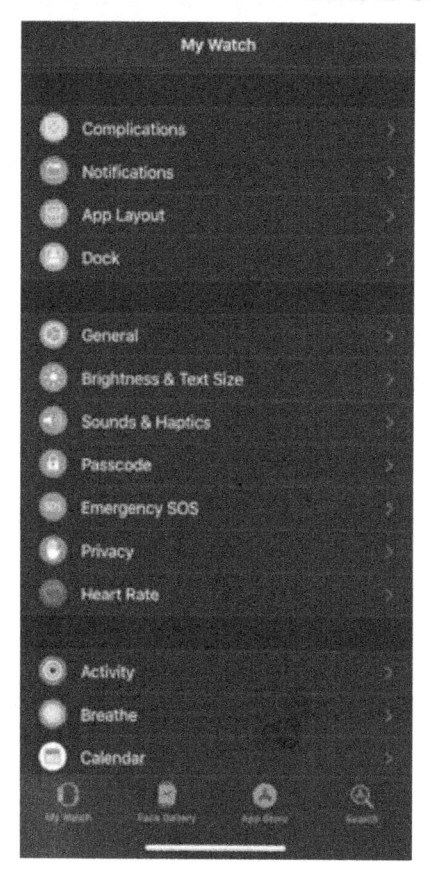

STATUS ICONS

Notifications on the Apple Watch come in many forms; one way is through status icons; these icons let you quickly glance down at your wrist and know there's a new email or your watch needs to be charged. Some are less obvious than others. The status icons and what they mean are listed below:

You have an unread notification such as an email.

⚡

The Apple Watch is charging.

⚡

Your battery is low.

🔒

The Apple Watch is locked and needs a passcode to use.

🌙

Your watch is in Do Not Disturb mode and will not make any sounds or light up until enabled again; alarms, however, will still work.

✈

The Apple Watch is in Airplane mode and only non-wireless features work—Bluetooth and Wi-Fi are not turned on.

🎭

Your watch is in Theater mode and stays silent and the screen stays dark, unless you tap on the screen or press one of the buttons.

📶

Your watch is connected to a Wi-Fi network instead of your phone.

●●●●

This is something you'll only see on an Apple Watch with a cellular connection. It indicates you are connected to cellular; the bars indicate how strong the connection is. Four is the highest.

✕

Again, this is only something you'll see on an Apple Watch with a cellular connection, and it means you have lost your cellular connection.

If you are swimming or doing something with lots of water, this indicates that water lock is on, and the watch will not respond to taps.

Swipe up to your Glances and you'll see this icon; it represents your audio connection. Tapping on this will let you switch audio from your watch to another device. So, for instance, if you are listening to music and want it to play on a wireless headset.

Location service is on. What does this mean? It means there's an app (such as Maps) that's using your location in the background.

Your watch is no longer paired with your phone.

There's wireless activity happening or some other kind of active event—an app loading, for example.

If you are using the Workout app, then you'll see this status icon appear. Tap it to switch back to the app.

I'll cover the Walkie-Talkie feature later; for now, just understand that this icon represents that feature.

You'll see this icon when audio is playing.

When you are using a third-party app for driving directions or navigation, you'll see this status icon.

Sometimes your watch is listening—for example, if your watch detects you are washing your hands, then this icon will pop up to tell you the mic is on and the watch is now listening to what you are doing (detecting the water, in that example).

If you have activated Sleep mode, then you'll see this status icon anytime you have gone to bed for the night. You can toggle it on manually by swiping up to get to the Glances screen and tapping on the icon.

Gestures and Shortcuts

With such a limited space, Apple really made use of something called Gestures. Gestures is essentially your watch doing different things based on how you touch or swipe the watch. If you have an iPhone or Mac with Force Touch, you'll be somewhat familiar with this. If not, don't worry—it's easy to understand.

This section will give you a quick overview of the gestures and shortcuts that let you do what you need to do quickly.

The Big Three

There are three actions that you'll use more than others.

#1

The one shortcut you will use the most is the Digital Crown knob; pressing it will always get you back to the Home screen. It's like the Home button on your iPhone (if you have an iPhone that still has a Home screen button).

#2

Swiping down from the top edge of your watch face will get you notifications. If you missed a text, email or any other alert, then swipe down and you can see what it was. You probably know this gesture is exactly the same as your iPhone—Apple, whenever possible, tries to keep gestures the same or similar.

If you swipe left over a notification, you'll get two more options: clear and more options.

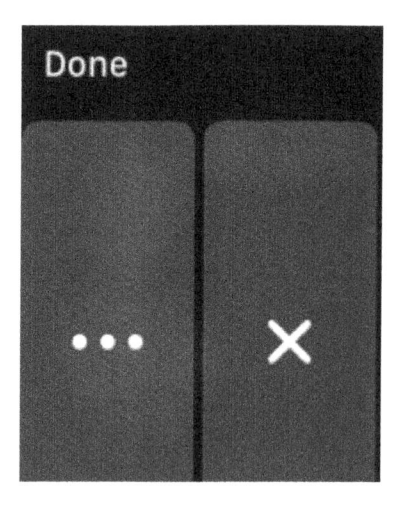

Clear does exactly what it sounds like—it clears! More options lets you change how a notification is delivered.

Notifications can start adding up really quickly. Maybe you are the type who loves to go through each one and clear them individually; I find it time-consuming and would rather clear them at once. That's easy! Just tap and hold on any notification (that means you touch it firmly and hold until a message pops up). When the Clear All message comes up, tap it. This won't delete the message—only the notification.

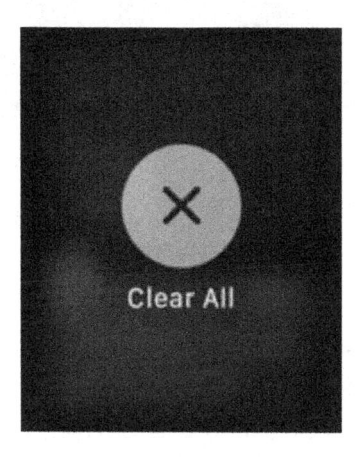

#3

Swipe up from the bottom edge of your watch face to see Glances. Glances is a little like the Control Center on your iPhone—on older iPhones it's the same gesture to get there (swiping up); newer iPhones access this by swiping down at the upper right corner.

Glances

Glances are nothing more than shortcuts and toggles. All those status icons I just mentioned? A lot of them are turned on here.

So when you want Swim mode or Airplane mode turned on, for example, just go into Glances and push the button. Push it again to turn it off. Some of the icons (like the battery percent icon) will open up more options.

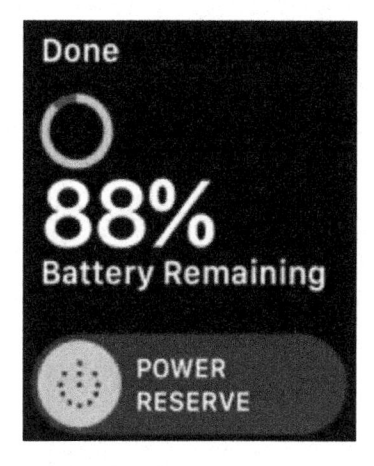

One status icon not covered previously was the flashlight, which is one of the Glance options. On your iPhone, the flashlight is pretty useful (and bright); on the watch? Not so much. On the watch, the display turns on, so you have "some" light, but it's not the same brightness as using your camera's flash like on the phone. Swiping it will bring up the different kinds of flashlights (white, flashing white, and red). To turn it off, swipe down.

At the bottom of Glances, there's an Edit button. If you tap that, you'll be able to drag and drop icons around; this way you can organize the icons in order of the ones you use the most.

You can also tap the – button in the upper left corner of each icon to remove it from Glances. You can't remove every icon, but you can remove most of them.

When you remove it, it's not gone for good. You can get it back by going to the bottom; it will show up under More.

Force Touch

For quite some time, Apple promoted Force Touch as an innovation in gestures—and then it didn't. And now it's gone!

Force Touch would measure not just what you are touching, but how hard you are touching it. On your watch / clock screen, pressing a little harder on the screen will let you change the watch face. In apps, Force Touch is used a bit like right-clicking on a computer—it brings up options.

Apple has since decided to hide this feature entirely. So if you are wondering why pressing more firmly no longer brings up a menu, that's why.

Zooming

You may be used to pinching and zooming on your iPhone and iPad; be prepared to be disappointed...on a smaller screen this method just doesn't work. In its place is the Digital Crown, which can be used to zoom in and out by turning the knob. You can use it to magnify things like photos and maps.

Turning off the Screen

There's no physical button to turn off the Apple Watch. To turn the screen off you can either put your hand down or cover the watch with your other hand. You can also silence alarms by covering your hand over the screen.

Launching Siri

There are two quick ways to launch Siri: one, press and hold the Digital Crown; two, lift up your wrist and speak—no buttons are required. Previously, you'd have to say "Hey Siri"; that's no longer needed. The watch can detect you lifting your wrist to speak and hears what you say.

You can also use Siri for translations. Just say "Hey Siri, how do you say X [thing] in Y [language]?"

Locate your iPhone

If you can't find your iPhone, you can quickly ping it with your watch to see if it's nearby. Go to your watch face, swipe up to bring up Glances, then tap the Phone icon.

This will make your phone start beeping. (Note: for this to work you must enable Find My iPhone from iCloud.)

Airplane Mode

Most airlines will let you leave your watch on while you're flying, but they will want it in Airplane mode (which turns off settings that might interfere with the plane).

To put the watch in Airplane mode, go to your watch face, swipe up from the bottom to bring up Glances, and go to the Settings glance, then tap the button that looks like an airplane. Repeat the steps to turn the mode off.

If you'd like the watch to go in Airplane mode whenever your phone does, then go to the Apple Watch app, tap My Watch, then tap Airplane mode and turn on Mirror iPhone. Repeat the steps to disable.

SIDE BUTTON

To toggle between your most recently used apps, press the side button on from the watch face. This brings up all the apps like a rolodex. It's kind of like multitasking on an iPhone.

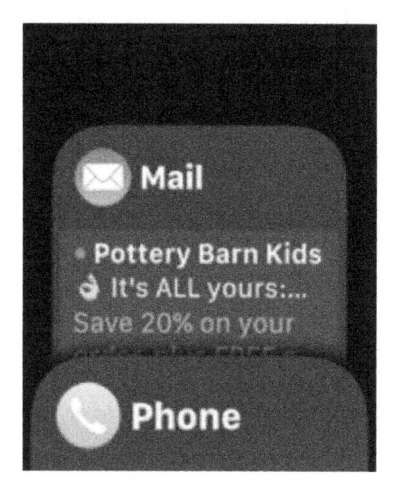

Use the Digital Crown to scroll through them; tap once to open an app; swipe right to crash the app.

LAST APP

Need to go back to the last app used quickly? Double click the Digital Crown.

Apple Pay

To use Apple Pay, double tap the side button; it will come up with your credit card and tell you to put it near the reader (your phone does not need to be nearby); once it is by the reader, you enter your passcode. Worried about someone taking your watch and using your credit card? It won't work when it's taken off your wrist.

If you want to use a different credit card, swipe to the left. When you find the card you want, turn it to face the reader. When the transaction goes through, you'll hear a beep and you'll feel a tap—this alerts you to the fact that the transaction is complete.

Before you can use Apple Pay, however, you need to set it up. This is done on the iPhone. From your iPhone, tap the Apple Watch app, and then scroll to Add Credit or Debit Card, and then tap it. You can either use a card on file with iTunes or add a new card. In either case, you'll have to add your security number (or the full number if you are adding a new card); depending on the card, you may need to verify with another step, which is usually a text message with a code from your bank. When you get the code, just tap Verify and enter it. You're all set to use your watch to buy things!

Handoff Between the Apple Watch and iPhone

Handoff lets you toggle between your watch and your phone without losing your place. If you are reading an email on your watch, and want to reply on your phone, then go to Handoff on your phone. Handoff used to appear on the Lock screen —it's a little less obvious now. You now access Handoff from your app switcher screen on the iPhone (see below). Just swipe up and hold on your iPhone.

On a MacBook, Handoff is in the dock. It will have an Apple Watch icon in the upper right corner.

You can turn Handoff on and off by opening the Apple Watch app on your iPhone, going to My Watch, then tapping on General, and Enable Handoff.

Arranging Icons

There are two app views on the Apple Watch: Grid View and List View.

Grid View

Grid View is the view that most people are used to; it's also tiny…really tiny. When you have a lot of apps, it can be difficult to find the one you want. If you find it hard to navigate, then List View can help.

List View

List View puts all the apps in a scrollable list that's in alphabetical order.

REMOVING APPS

If you are using Grid View, then you can remove an app from the grid the same way you would on the Home screen of your iPhone or iPad: tap and hold. The apps that are removable will have little X's in the upper right corner. Tap those X's to remove them.

It will confirm that you really want to delete it before it takes it away. It's not gone for good; it's just stored in the cloud. You can put it back later.

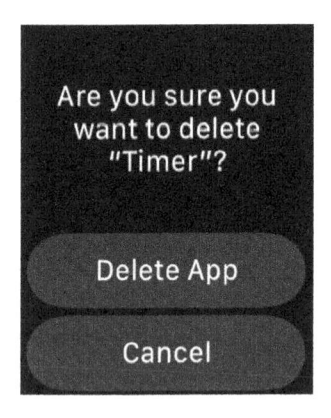

Arranging Icons

Arranging icons on the watch is also similar to the iPhone and iPad. To start, go to your Home screen, then touch and hold an app icon; you can now drag it to a new location.

Switching App Views

To switch from Grid View to List View (or vice versa), go to the Settings app, then scroll to App View.

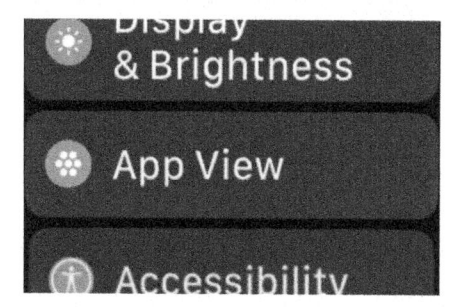

From the next screen, select the view that you want. Press the digital crown when you make your selection.

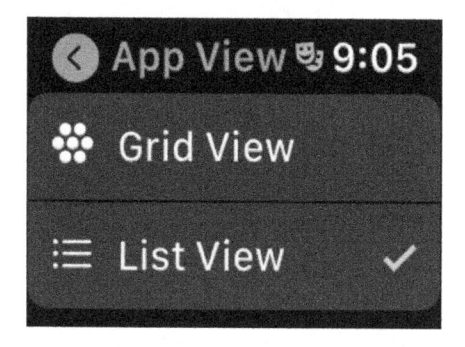

Installing Apps on The Watch

The days of using your phone to find and download apps are over with OS 7. True, you can still use the method referenced in the above section, and you may actually prefer it because it's easier to navigate and browse.

To find apps directly on your watch and skip the old method, open the Apps app on your watch.

This brings up a watch version of the App Store; you can either search for apps or use the Digital Crown to look through featured apps.

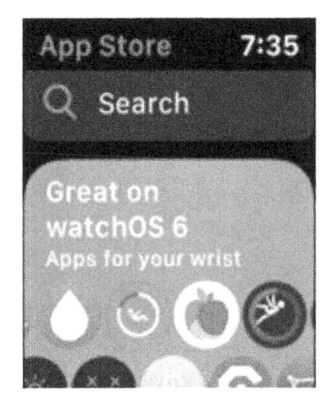

When you see an app that you want, tap it, then tap the Get button.

SOS

SOS allows your watch to call local emergency services to tell them your location; this is obviously something you only use in an emergency—it's not something to try out just to see how it works! To enable it, hold the side button for three seconds, and then swipe SOS.

Noise

Series 4 and up watches will have a new app appear after updating to OS 7: the Noise app.

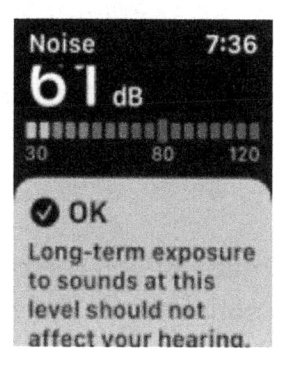

The Noise app uses the microphone in your watch to measure the sound levels of your environment. When it raises to a level that can harm your hearing, it can notify you.

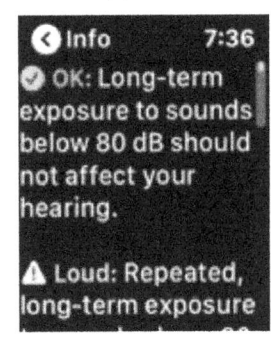

To turn it on, open the app and select enable.

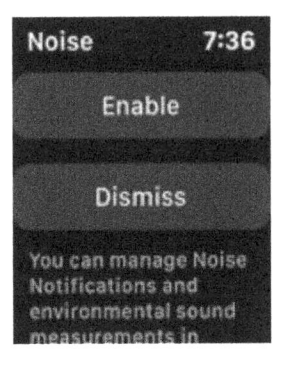

Once it's turned on, you can open it at any time to measure the sound level. You can also adjust when you get notifications about the sound levels by going into Settings on your watch, then Noise, then Notifications.

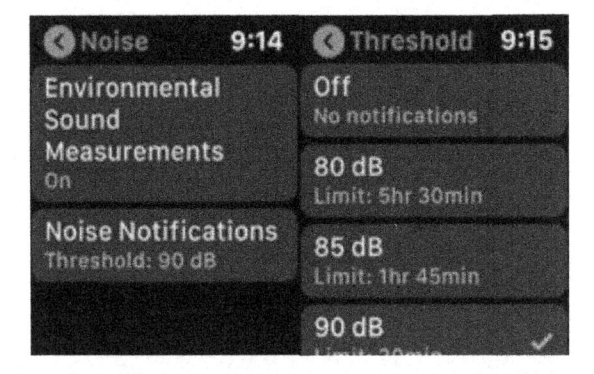

If you are listening to something too loud, you'll get a message about how repeated noise at this level can damage your hearing.

To see a history of noises, open the Health app on your iPhone.

Inside the app, tap the Browse icon on the bottom.

In the list, select the option for Hearing.

You will now see a chart history of noises you have been exposed to.

Breathe

Breathe was introduced on the WatchOS 3 Home screen. It's a free relaxation app designed to help calm your body after a workout or stressful day at work.

Compass

The compass is an app that's exclusive to Apple Watch Series 5 and up. Older watches don't have this app.

The compass is pretty much what you would expect: it shows the direction the watch is facing along with the current location and elevation. You can use the Digital Crown to see your incline and other coordinates. Firmly pressing on the display will let you edit your bearings.

[6]
Let's Make Faces…Apple Watch Faces, That Is!

This chapter will cover:
- What is an Apple Watch face?
- How to change the Apple Watch face
- How to customize different Apple Watch faces
- Adding complications to a watch face
- Watch faces
- How to share a face
- Find more faces
- Remove a face

One of the things that really makes an Apple Watch stand out is how personal the watch face is. When the original Apple Watch launched, there weren't even a dozen watch faces; today there are several dozen. Within each face, there are countless ways to customize them and add complications to them (a watch complication is basically a function within the watch face—for example, in addition to telling time, the watch face gives you the weather or surfing condition).

In this chapter we'll look at how to change faces, share faces, and what the official watch faces are.

To get started, let's see how to change a face. It's simple: press and hold the face for about three seconds.

This will pull back your face a little, and show you the title of the face, and give you the option to edit it and to share it. We'll look at editing and sharing later in this chapter. For now, swipe left and right to see the different faces.

It's not going to show you all the faces at this point. It's going to show you the ones that you've been using. If you're new to the Apple Watch, then it will be pretty sparse.

To see all of the faces, swipe to the left until you get to the large + button, then tap it.

This will bring up a long list of watch faces; use your finger to drag up and down, or use the Digital Crown on your watch.

Watch Faces and What They Do

Every face has different details that can be added or removed. Below is a list of the current watch faces and what you can add to them. Watch faces that have status icons can be touched to load the associated app. (Note: not all of these faces will be on earlier watch models; additionally, some are only available to watch models with cellular.)

Activity Analog / Activity Digital

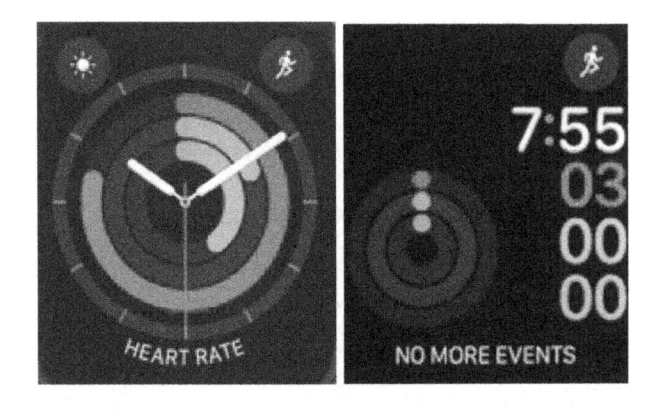

This is the face to use when working out. It measures your progress but has an overlay of a clock to give you the time as well. There are two versions: analog with no numbers; and digital with numbers.

Artist

This face is a collaboration between Apple and the artist Geoff McFetridge. McFetridge is a Canadian born artist who currently is based out of Los Angeles, California. He's known for his bold colors and simplistic designs. He has worked for brands like Nike and Patagonia, and also did the title sequence for the films "The Virgin Suicides" and "Adaptation."

Stripes

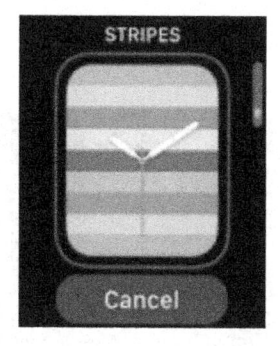

This face includes different striped patterns. The idea is to use these colored patterns to create sports teams or flag colors.

I'll cover customizing faces below, but briefly, this is one of the more complicated faces to customize because of the number of options.

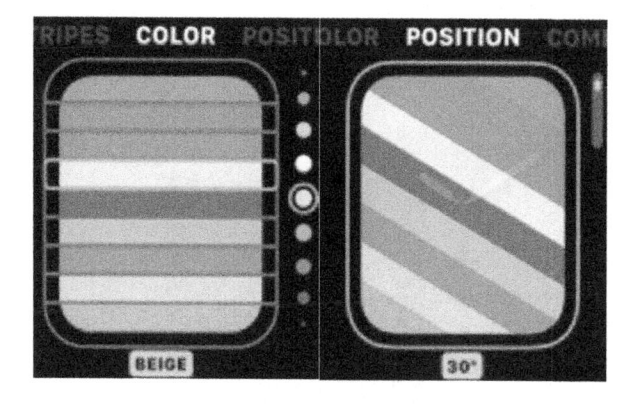

When you edit the face, you can select a unique color for each line, and change the position, so it can appear horizontally, vertically, or at an angle.

BREATHE

Unleash the yogi inside you. This simplistic watch face has one goal: encouraging you to breathe.

CALIFORNIA

California turns your face into a more traditional watch face. There are lots of customizations here; you can go from full screen to a circular face, for example, by going into customizations, then turning your Digital Crown on the full screen menu.

Memoji

Brings animated Memoji's (covered in greater detailed in the next section) to the watch face.

Mickey Mouse

Featuring Mickey Mouse (and now Minnie Mouse), this is certainly the most whimsical and animated watch experience. Tap him and he will speak the time—if sound is on. The following can be added to the face: date, calendar, moon phase, sunrise / sunset, weather, activity summary, alarm, timer, stopwatch, battery charge, world clock, and stocks.

TOY STORY

Not to be outdone by the Mickey face, is the Toy Story face. Tap the screen to get a different animation.

GRADIENT

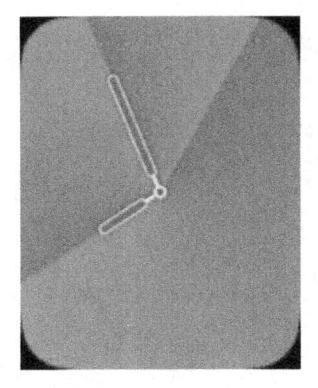

Gradient is a very simple face that will slightly change as time passes.

MERIDIAN

A classic look with four subdials.

MODULAR / MODULAR COMPACT

A very modern-looking face with lots of room to add things. Color can be adjusted, and the following features can be added: calendar, moon phase, sunrise /sunset, weather, stocks, activity summary, alarm, timer, stopwatch, battery charge, world clock. There are two versions of this face: Modular and Modular Compact.

Motion

This is one of the few Apple Watch faces that is fully animated. You can pick between a butterfly, flower, and jellyfish. The following can be added to the face: date.

NUMERALS / NUMERALS DUO / NUMERALS MONO

Numerals has three unique designs (normal, Duo, and Mono) with several customizations. The basic design shows the time in a bold and easy-to-read way.

COUNT UP

Tapping on the bezel of this app lets you quickly start tracking the time elapsed.

Simple

As the name implies, this is the simplest classic watch face. The following can be adjusted on the face: color of the sweep hand and the numbering of the dial. The following can be added: date, calendar, moon phase, sunrise / sunset, weather, activity summary, alarm, timer, stopwatch, battery charge, and world clock.

Solar / Solar Graph

Bring out your inner scientist with this face, which displays the sun's position in the sky.

UTILITY

A very basic and classic looking face; the following features can be changed: the color of the second hand and the numbering on the dial. The following can be added to the face: date, calendar, moon phase, sunrise / sunset, weather, activity summary, alarm, timer, stopwatch, batter charge, world clock, and stocks.

GMT

The idea of this face is to show multiple time zones at the same time. A 12-hour time is shown on the inner dial (with time where you are located); the outer later shows a 24-hour time.

X-Large

X-Large is the most simplistic modern face—it's also the boldest looking. The following can be adjusted: color.

Explorer

This face is a cellular exclusive. The goal of the watch face is to show you the cell signal strength.

Fire and Water / Vapor

Animates with smoke whenever you lift it.

Typograph

Displays three styles (custom, modern, and rounded) along with four different scripts (Arabic, Arabic Indic, Devanagari, and Roman).

INFOGRAPH / INFOGRAPH MODULAR

This was an Apple Watch Series 4 exclusive face; it gives you a wealth of info at your wrist—time in another city, UVI index, weather, etc.

If you updated your watch or got a new one, then you might be a bit surprised to see it's now a

B&W face. Not to worry! Color is still there and it's a quick fix—just press and hold, then select customize, then use your Digital Crown to scroll to Multicolor, then press your Digital Crown twice.

Kaleidoscope

The face changes patterns based on your preferences.

Liquid Metal

Animates with melting metal whenever you lift your wrist.

Pride / Pride Analog

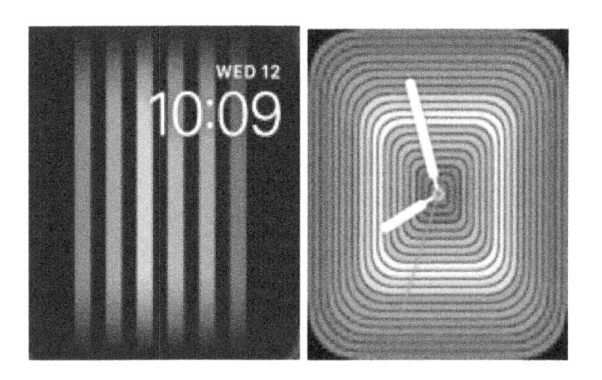

Celebrating Pride colors has long been a face on the Apple Watch; starting with OS 6 and continuing in OS 7, a new analog face is included.

Astronomy

This watch face shows you the exact position of different planets and displays day, date and time.

Chronograph (Pro)

A very precise and classic watch face that includes a stopwatch that can be activated from the watch face. The following can be adjusted: dial details and face color. You can also add the following to the face: date, moon phase, sunrise / sunset, calendar, weather, stocks, activity summary, alarm, timer, battery charge, and world clock.

COLOR

A very basic face whose primary feature is to change colors. The following can be adjusted: dial color. The following can be added to the face: date, moon phase, sunrise / sunset, weather, activity summary, stopwatch, timer, battery charge, world clock, and your monogram.

SIRI

The Siri face doesn't look like what you might expect; you think Siri and you might think of those waves that appear when you say "Hey Siri"; the watch face takes a look at your day (like your calendar appointments, traffic and weather) and displays it in an organized way; you can turn your Digital Crown to see more events.

SOLAR DIAL

This face features a 24-hour dial that tracks the sun; the dial (either analog or digital) moves opposite the sun's path.

Timelapse

Features time-lapse videos that change from morning, afternoon, and night as time passes (you can also use your Digital Crown to move it); you can pick between natural and cityscape landscape. At this writing, the landscapes include: Mack Lake, New York, Hong Kong, London, Paris, and Shanghai.

Photos

The best watch face for last in many people's opinion: photos. Photos lets you show a slideshow of photos and the time. So every time you lift your wrist, something new awaits. Live photos even have animations!

To add this face, swipe all the way to the left of all the watch faces, and then tap New.

Now scroll down to Photos, and tap once.

If you want to show only one particular photo, then open the Photos app on your watch.

Scroll to the photo you want. In the photo below, you'll see an icon in the lower right corner of a circle with dots—this indicates that the photo is a live photo and will be animated as an Apple Watch face.

Once it's on the screen, firm press. This will bring up an option to make it the watch face.

You can make it a normal watch face, or an abstract one (kaleidoscope).

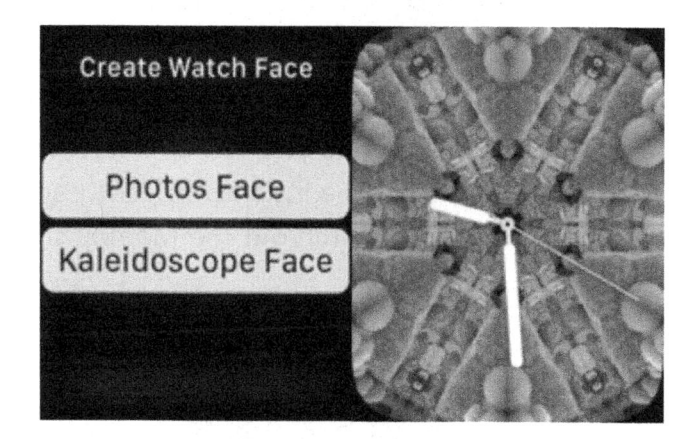

If you want to remove a watch face, just go to change the face as you normally would and swipe up.

Editing a Watch Face

Every watch face has different customizations; some have very little you can change, and some have dozens of things.

To make changes to a face, tap and hold it for three seconds, then select Edit.

As an example, I'll show a Memoji face just because there's a lot of edits you can do here. Notice on the right side, there's a little scroll? You can drag up or down and switch out the Memoji character.

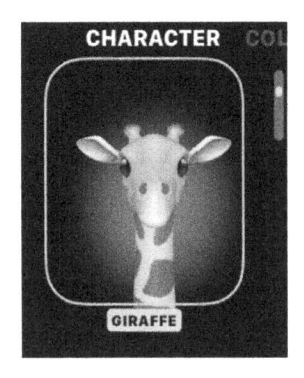

Once you find the character you want, you can drag to the right one time to be in the Color menu. You now can select a background color on the right side.

Swipe right again, and you'll see the available complications. Not all complications are available on this face.

Once I'm happy with my changes, I can press the Digital Crown to save them.

Sharing a Watch Face

If you spend several minutes creating a watch face, then you are probably pretty proud, right?! Why not share it?

To share, press the face for three seconds to bring up the option menu, then tap the share button to the left of the Edit button.

Once you tap share, it will bring up a Message; tap Add Contact to select who you are sharing it with. Under Create Message, you can write a message or leave it blank.

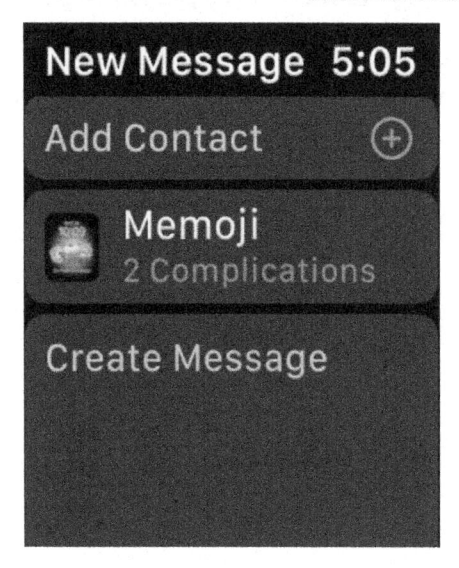

Once you are satisfied, scroll down and tap Send.

Finding a Watch Face

If you want to add a new face that isn't in the list of faces, you have two options.

If you know the name of the face, then go to the App Store on your watch and search for it.

The second option is to go to the website where the face is, and tap add to watch

Removing a Watch Face

Once you start adding faces, you might find that you have too many and it takes too long to switch between them.

You can quickly remove a face by holding on the watch face, swiping to the face you want to remove, and then swiping up. This will bring up a confirmation about removing the face. Just tap remove and it's gone.

Making Changes on Your iPhone

So we've seen how to change a face on the Apple Watch; it's pretty easy. But it's also pretty small. If you find it's difficult, there's a second option: use your iPhone.

When you open the Apple Watch app, you'll see all your watch faces right at the top. You can swipe left and right just as you would on your watch.

If you want to edit the face, just tap on it once. All the changes you could make on your watch are here, but they're a little easier to see because there's more screen real estate.

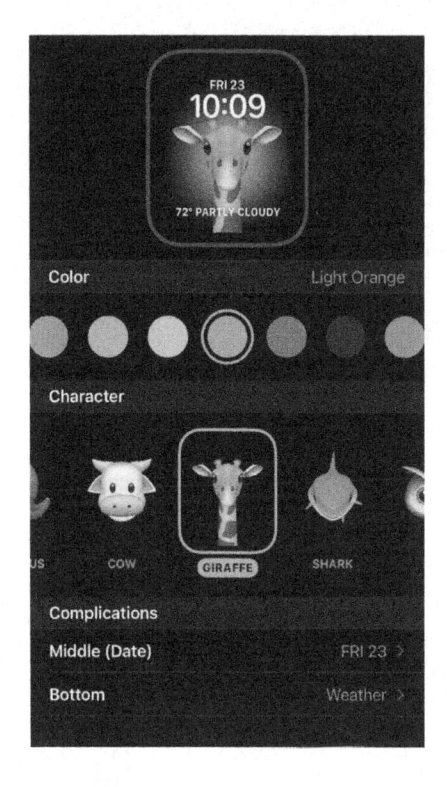

Once you make your changes, just scroll down and tap Set as current Watch Face (assuming it's not the watch face already); changes are all automatically synced.

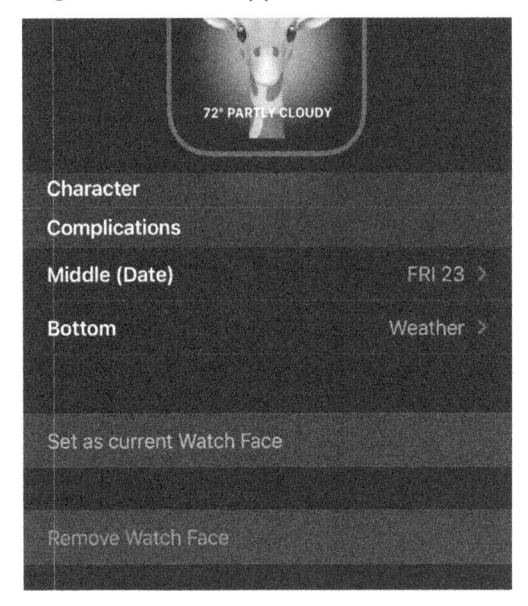

You can even share your watch face right from your phone. Just tap the face you want to share and tap the share button in the upper right corner.

This will bring up a pull up menu asking how you want to share it—you can email it, send it to Slack, text message it, or more.

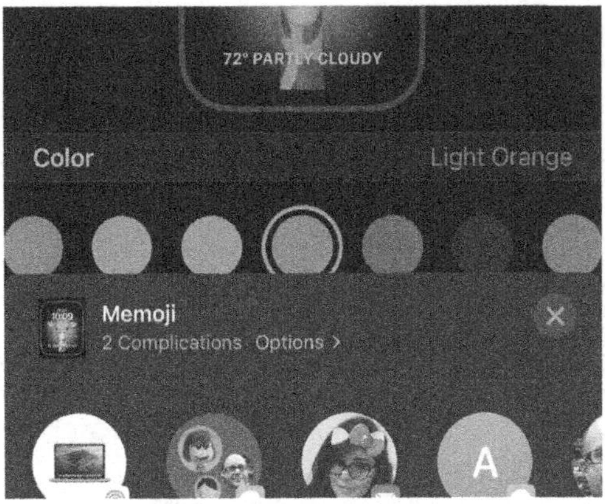
72° PARTLY CLOUDY
Color
Light Orange
Memoji
2 Complications Options ›
A

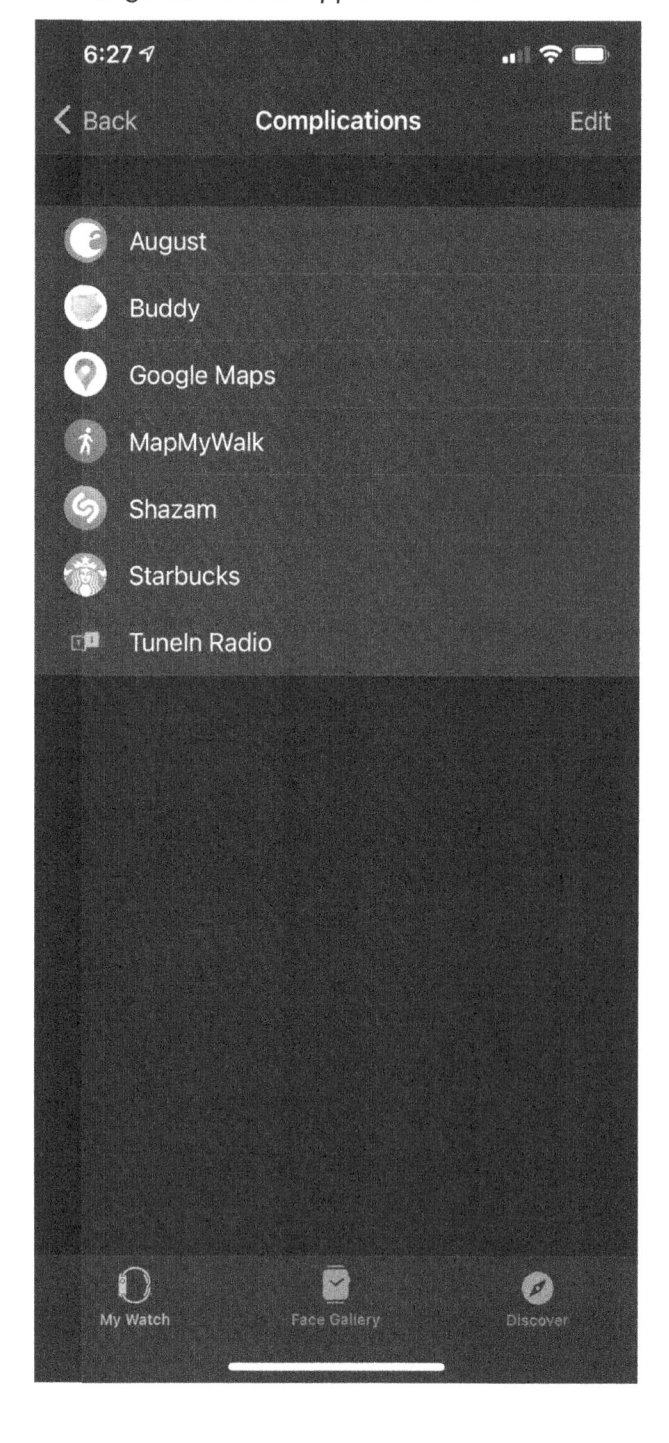

- August
- Buddy
- Google Maps
- MapMyWalk
- Shazam
- Starbucks
- TuneIn Radio

Scott La Counte | 111

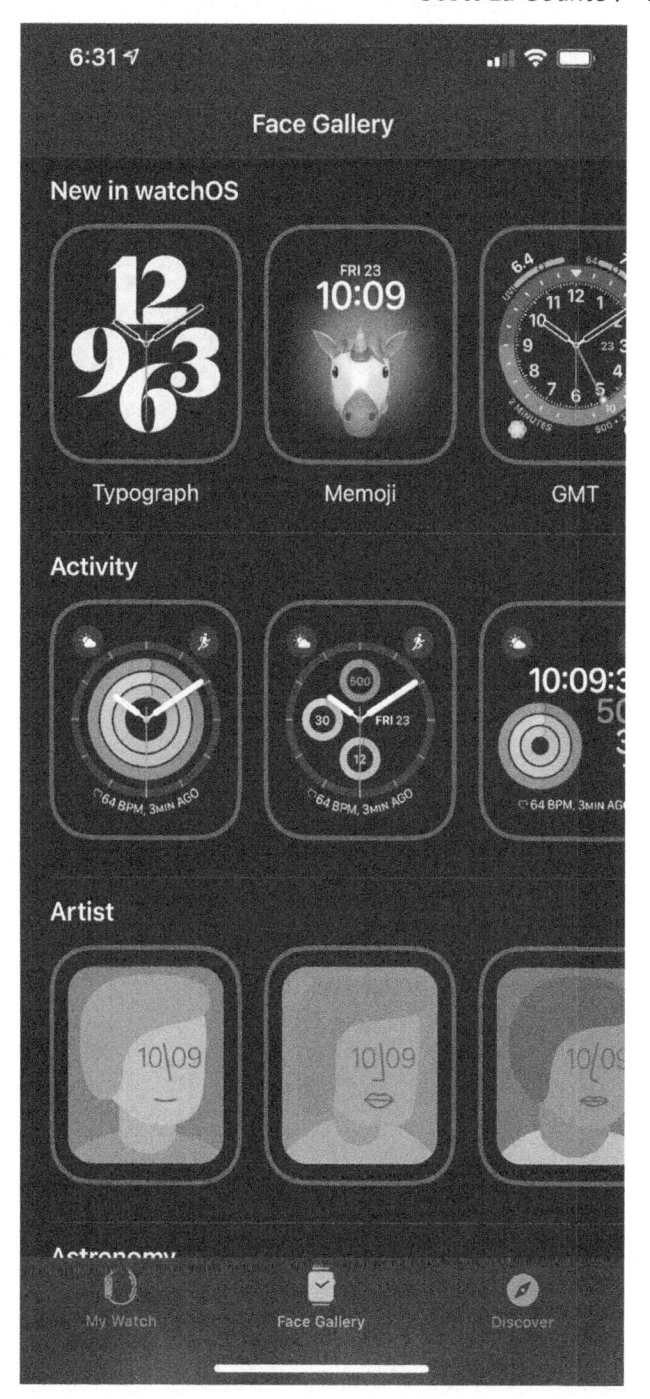

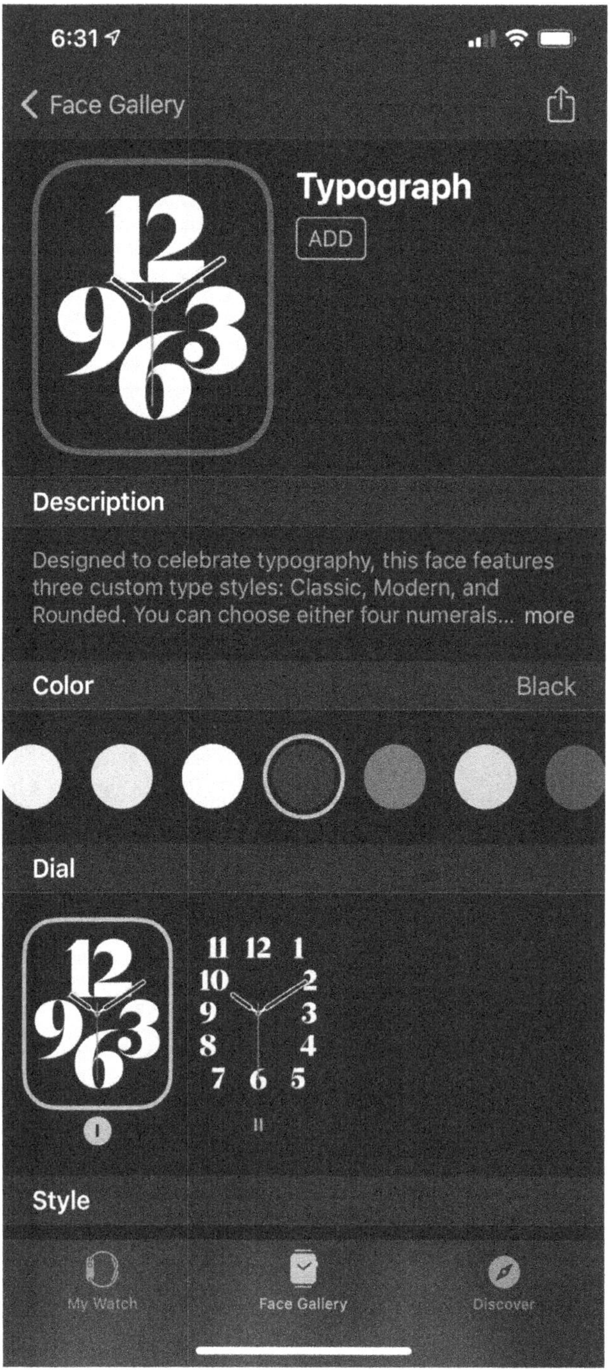
6:31
Face Gallery
Typograph
ADD
Description
Designed to celebrate typography, this face features three custom type styles: Classic, Modern, and Rounded. You can choose either four numerals... more
Color
Black
Dial
I
II
Style
My Watch
Face Gallery
Discover

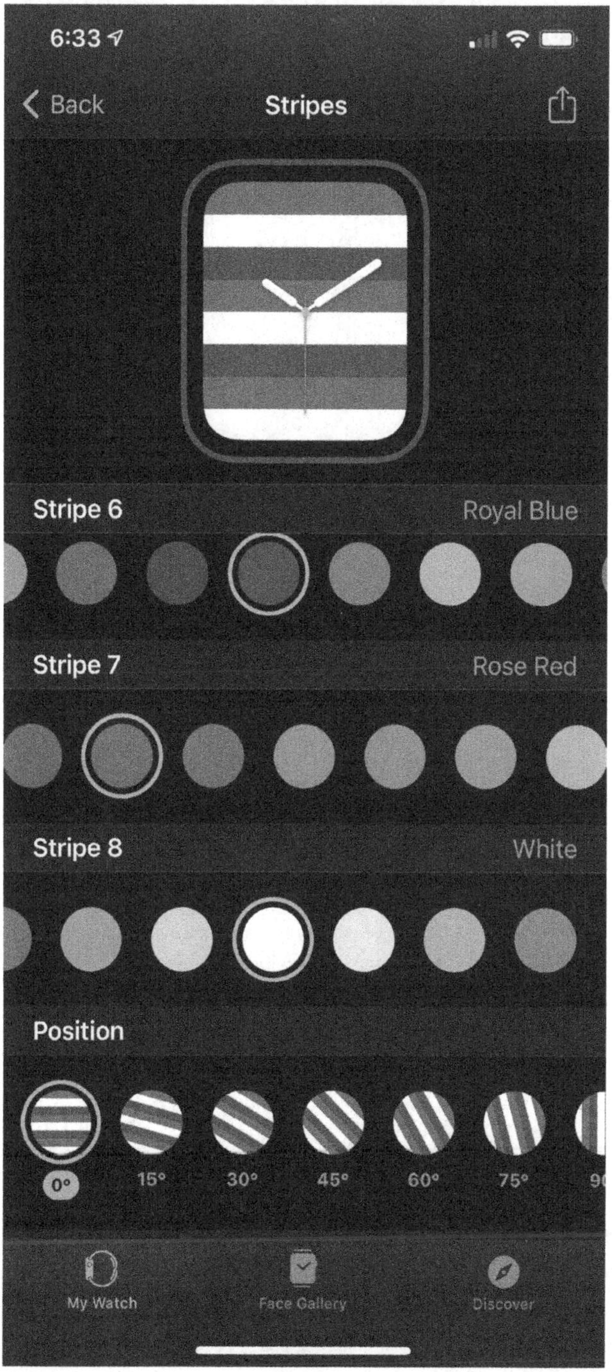
6:33
Back
Stripes
Stripe 6
Royal Blue
Stripe 7
Rose Red
Stripe 8
White
Position
0°
15°
30°
45°
60°
75°
My Watch
Face Gallery
Discover

114 | *Getting Started With Apple Watch SE*

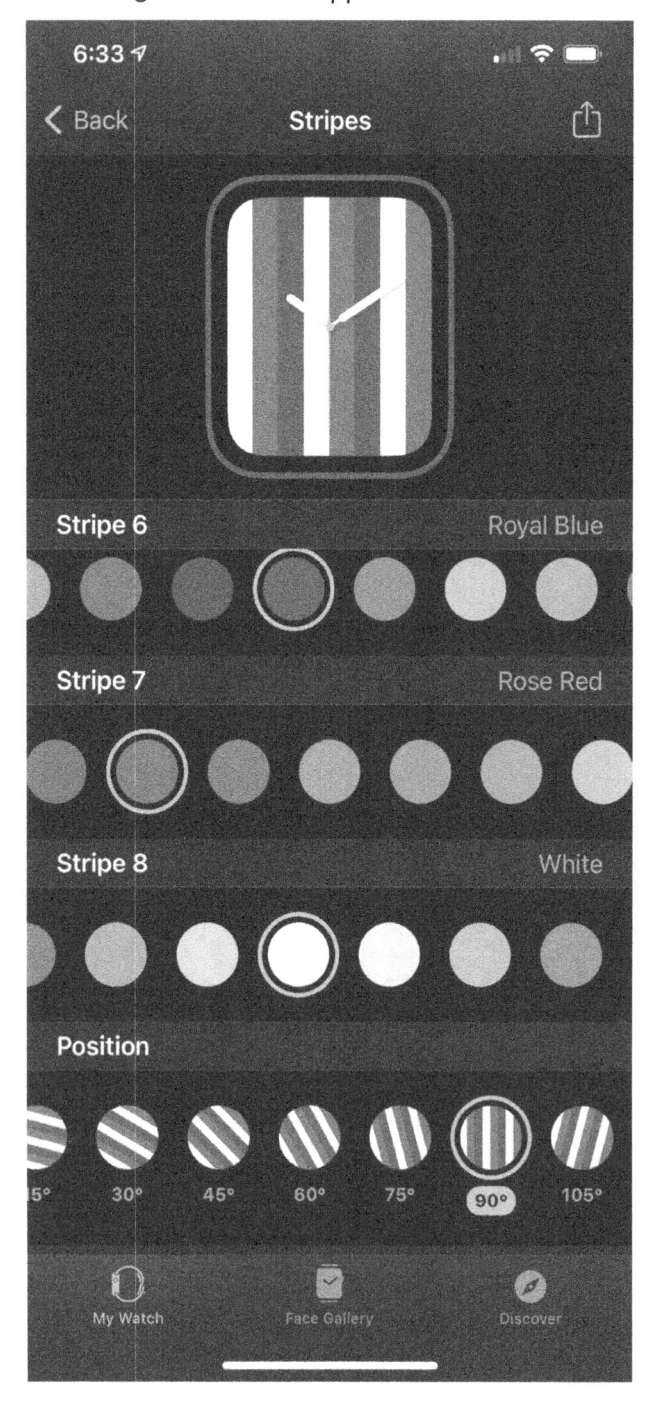

[7]
SHOW ME WHAT THIS WATCH IS CAPABLE OF…BUT KEEP IT RIDICULOUSLY SIMPLE

This chapter will cover:
- Creating a Memoji
- Sending / receiving messages
- Reading / sending email
- Using Siri
- Making phone calls
- Washing your hands
- Adding calendar events
- Setting reminders

- Using the map
- Using photos
- Listening to music
- Looking up the weather
- Setting alarms and timers
- Using the Apple Watch with the Apple TV
- Using the Apple Watch as a Walkie-Talkie

Memoji

If you've never created a Memoji on your phone, you are missing out. They are fun and better shown than explained. In the simplest terms, however: they are avatars that you can send to express yourself.

You can now create an Memoji right on your watch. To get started, open the Memoji app.

If you have Memoji's on your phone already, then you'll see them here. You can tap them to edit them. To create a new Memoji, tap the big + icon.

The first thing you'll see is a bald icon. You can scroll through a pretty long list of things you can change: skin, hairstyle, brows, eyes, head, nose, mouth, ears, facial hair, eyewear, and headwear.

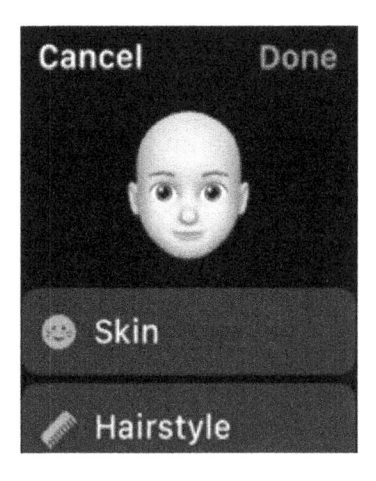

Each thing you select will have submenus for even more things you can change. On the example below, you'll notice it says "Color" then next to it, it says Freckles? Just swipe horizontally to go to the next submenu.

Under headwear, you can even select if you want your Memoji to wear a face covering.

When you are done, select Done. If you decide to change something later, just tap on the Emoji and select from the menu what you want to change.

Create a Memoji Watch Face

You can also use your Memoji as a watch face. Just go to the Memoji app, tap the Memoji you want to use as a watch face, and select "Create Watch Face."

Once you create it, it will look a little like the below; each time you lift your wrist, it will have a different expression.

Deleting a Memoji

If you want to delete a Memoji, just open the Memoji app, tap the avatar you want to delete, scroll to the bottom, and tap Delete.

Using Memoji in a Message

I'll cover Messages in the next section, but very quickly, I'll point out that you can now use any Memoji you create in a message.

To do it, open the Message app, then tap the Memoji button when you reply.

You'll see a list of all your Memoji stickers. Tap the avatar you want to use.

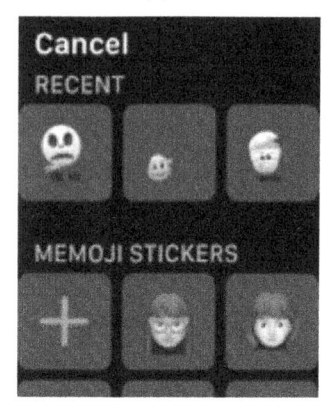

Next, tap the type of expression you want to apply.

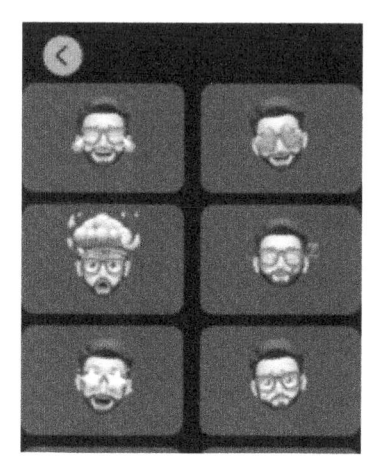

You'll see the Memoji in your message reply now.

Using Memoji on the iPhone

Once you create a Memoji worthy of an art gallery, how do you use it on your phone? Easy! Open the message app—it's already there! It automatically syncs.

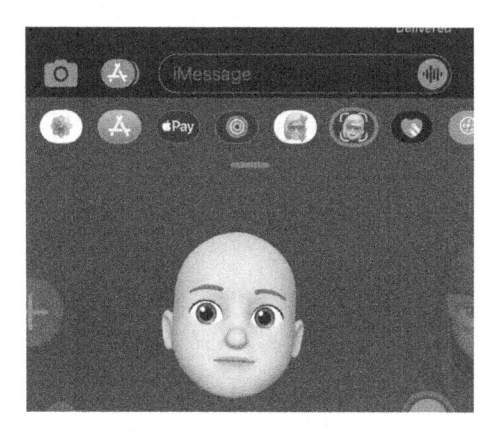

Messages

The first thing you should know about Messages is this isn't the place to type an epic love note. It's the place where you send quick replies. Technically you could do something a little grander, but the time and effort involved makes it rather fruitless.

To begin a new message, go to your watch's Home screen and open the Messages app. Then select New Message.

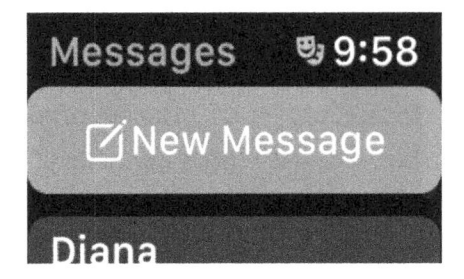

From here, tap Add a Contact. Once you pick your contact, tap Create Message.

There are a few ways you can create a message. The first is to dictate it. When you dictate it, it listens to what you say and transcribes it—not always accurately (especially if it's noisy).

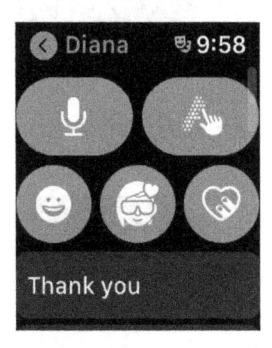

The second way is to scribble it. When you scribble it, you write the letters one at a time. If you need to change a letter, you can delete it, or tap it and scroll through more choices.

Next is the message with taps (that's the icon with the heart and finger). This is good if you are trying to get the attention of someone else who is also wearing an Apple Watch. They feel whatever tap vibration you send them.

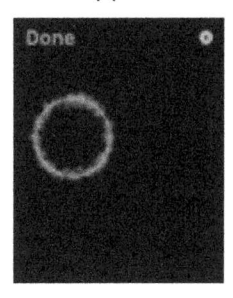

Finally, you can send an emoji and Memoji's.

Underneath the five ways to create messages are common phrases. Tap any of them and it will add it to the message.

When you receive a message, Apple Watch will tap you. Move your hand toward you and the message will appear automatically; once you put your hand down, it turns off again. Use the watch's side knob to scroll through the message. You'll have the same methods to reply that you did when I showed how to write a message (above).

The biggest difference is Apple Pay is an option now. Apple Pay lets you send money to someone. So if you are out to lunch with a friend, you can pay your share of the bill right from the watch.

If no reply is needed, then hit the Dismiss button instead of the Reply button.

If you are not getting messages on your watch, then chances are a setting is not enabled; you can change the Messages settings from the Apple Watch app on your iPhone.

READING AND SENDING EMAIL

When you get mail, you'll get a notification; but there's also an app for reading and managing your email. As it is on the iPhone, the email app is simply named "Mail."

To start, go to the app on your Home screen and tap on it. It looks pretty bare-bones, but there's a lot to it. You can scroll through your messages from within the app. To read a message, tap it.

At any time, you can continue reading the message on your iPhone by swiping up on the Mail icon in the lower left corner of your iPhone's Lock screen. (Note: handoff does need to be set up, so refer to how to set up handoff in this book if you haven't already.)

While Apple Watch does support HTML formats (including different fonts and font colors), it still might look a little off, so for complex messages, the iPhone is the best place to read them.

If it's a long message, you can use the Digital Crown knob to scroll through it.

When a message includes phone numbers or addresses, the watch will automatically recognize them and turn them into hyperlinks. Tapping on them will either bring up the Phone or Map app (depending on what the hyperlink is).

To reply to an email, you will need to use the iPhone to compose it.

Managing Mail

Flag an Email

When you are reading an email on the watch, you can press firmly on the display, and then tap Flag. You can also flag a message from your message list by swiping the message to the left, then tapping on More.

Mark as Unread

If you want to mark a message as unread, go to your message list, swipe left, tap More, and then tap Unread.

Delete an Email

If you want to delete a message, go to your message list, swipe left, tap More, and then tap Trash. (Note: if your email is set up to archive a message, then you'll see the Archive button instead of the Trash button.)

Selecting the Inboxes that Appear

You may not want all of your mail to appear on your watch. Let's say you have a work email, family email, and spam email, and you only want your family email to appear. If that's the case, then go to the Apple Watch app on your iPhone, tap My Watch, and then go to Mail and Include Mail. Specify which mailbox you do or do not want to appear.

Customize Alerts

If you want to change how you are alerted when you get mail (or if you don't want alerts at all), then go to the Apple Watch app on your iPhone, and tap My Watch, then turn on Mail Alerts and Show Alerts. "Sound" would be alerts that make noises and "Haptic" is alerts that vibrate.

Message List

If you find your email message list is simply too long, you can reduce the number of lines of the preview by going to the Apple Watch app, tapping on My Watch and then going to Mail and Message Preview; pick two lines of message, one line of message or no lines of a message.

Siri

If you love Siri on the iPhone, you're going to love her even more on your wrist. Don't love her? Give her a second chance because she got a little bit of an upgrade.

You can access Siri one of two ways (you'll quickly discover that there are multiple ways to do most tasks on the watch):
1. Press the Digital Crown knob.
2. Raise your wrist and speak (say goodbye to "Hey Siri"). Just state your request (e.g. "What's the weather in Paris?" "Who won last night's Yankee game?"); you can use Siri to open apps, set alarms, call friends—pretty much anything you can think of. With no on-board keyboard, Siri is more important than ever.

Making Phone Calls

While you may not go out and buy an Apple Watch to get your Dick Tracy on and make phone calls from your wrist, it's certainly a nice touch...and it's pretty simple to do.

Once your watch is in sync with your iPhone, you are ready to start making and receiving calls.

If a call comes in, you can mute it by placing your hand over the watch. If you want to send it to your phone or reply with a text, then move your finger over the Digital Crown and scroll to the bottom.

To answer the call, use the green button; to decline the call, press the red one. It's just like getting a call on your iPhone. Your watch will use a built-in microphone when you speak into it. It's not the best quality, but it gets the job done.

To make a call, you have two options:

Go to your Home screen and tap the Phone icon.

The other option is the easiest; that option is to use Siri. Just lift your wrist and say, "call PERSON'S NAME." If the wrong person is dialed, just hit the Hang Up button and if you do it quickly enough, the call won't go through.

Calendar

The Calendar app on Apple Watch shows events you've scheduled or been invited to today and for the next week. Apple Watch shows events for all calendars you use on your iPhone.

To view your calendar, open the Calendar app on your Home screen or app list; you can also tap on the day's date on the watch face if you've added that option.

There are three different calendar modes. To toggle between them, go to the Settings app, and tap Calendar.

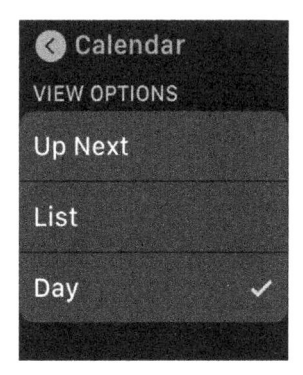

The first view is the Up Next view, which shows you a large view of any events you have—one event at a time. Tapping on any event will bring up event details and give you the option to edit it.

List View shows all your events in a collapsed view. Tapping on them enlarges the event and lets you edit it or see details.

Finally, the Today view shows you all the events on your calendar for a single day.

You can also see what's going on in your day by lifting your wrist and saying, "Siri, tell me what's going on today."

If you want to see the full month, then tap on the '<' in the upper left corner of the Calendar app, and then tap the monthly calendar; repeat the step to go back to Day view. When you are in Month view, any days that you have an activity will be highlighted in red.

Adding Events

To add an event, you will need to open the Calendar app on your iPhone. If you are in the Calendar app on your watch, then a Calendar icon will appear on your iPhone's Lock screen—just swipe up and it will go immediately to your calendar.

You can have Siri add an event for you.

Responding to Event Invites

When you get an invite to an event, it will appear as a notification; just swipe it or turn the Digital Crown knob when you see it, and then tap Accept, Maybe, or Decline.

The invite will also have the event organizer; to email the event organizer, press firmly on the display while you are looking at the event details; you will be able to either send them a voice message or call them.

To adjust any of your calendar's settings, go to the Apple Watch app on the iPhone, then tap My Watch, and finally tap Calendar.

Reminders

If you use reminders on the iPhone, then you might be disappointed to see there is no Reminders app on the Apple Watch.

Reminders, however, is sort of there; while no app exists, if you create a reminder on your iPhone through the Reminders app, it will also remind you on your watch.

You can also create a reminder on your watch by using Siri; just lift your wrist and say, "Hey Siri, set a reminder."

Map

There are a couple of ways to use the map on your Apple Watch; the easiest is to go to the Maps app on the list of apps. From here you'll see your current location and what's around you; you can use the Digital Crown knob to zoom in or out. To scroll / pan through the map, use your finger. If you tap the arrow in the bottom left corner, the current location will be updated.

To search the map, tap the three dots in the lower right corner.

This will pull up the option to either search for something or switch to a transit view. You obviously want Search Here.

This is going to bring up three options: dictate a location (the microphone icon), scribble a location (the finger icon), or search for a contact's address (the person icon). Underneath are also several nearby places to search—for example if you are looking for fast food, then tapping that will pull up a list of nearby fast food restaurants.

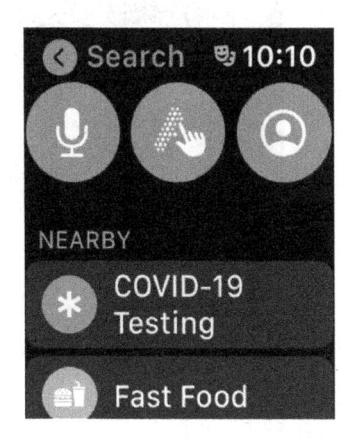

In the case of actual locations (businesses vs. just addresses) you'll also get information about hours.

Below this is the option to select the kind of directions that you want (along with the time it will take): walking, driving, transit, and cycling. Directions will change based on what you select—walking for example, will take you down streets that driving might not.

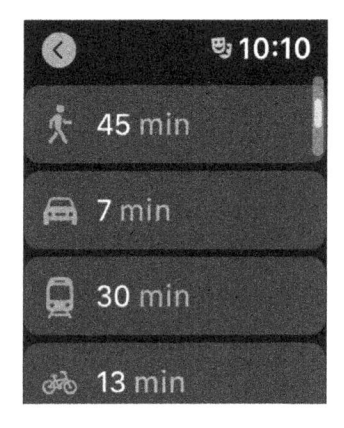

You can also stick a pin in an area that you want to go. To add a pin, just touch and hold Map (not firmly) and wait for the pin to drop. If you tap the pin after it's been dropped, it will give you the address. To move the pin, just hover over a new location and drop a new pin. If you aren't sure what someone's address is, if you drop a pin near their location you can get an approximate address.

Directions

Turn-by-turn directions on the Apple Watch is one of the bigger features, and it's really simple to use.

When you get a text with an address, the address is automatically converted to a hyperlink; click on it, and a map will immediately open. You can zoom in and out of the map by turning the Digital Crown knob.

If you don't have a message with the address, then go to your watch's Home screen, tap the Maps icon; the map will appear showing your current location. To find an address, tap your finger firmly on the screen. You'll get an option to either search for the address or use one of your contacts' addresses. When you search for an address, it will give you the option to use a recently used address or speak the address through dictation.

When the address comes up, there will be two options: driving directions and walking directions. Walking will not only change the time it will take, but also take you down paths a car cannot go. Once you make your selection by tapping, just hit the Start button.

One of the cool features about the map is the turn-by-turn directions. When it's time to make a turn, your watch will tap you to get your attention. Even more cool is if you start directions on your phone, it will also appear on your watch.

Photos

To view photos on the Apple Watch, go to the Photos app on your watch Home screen; because the watch cannot actually take photos, the photos you see will be the ones from your iPhone album. By default, the watch is set to display only your Favorites album, but you can change this.

Once the app is open, just tap the photo you want to view and use the Digital Crown knob to zoom in or out and use your finger to pan. Zoom all the way out to see all of your photos.

Pick an Album

If you'd like to choose another album to show on your watch, then open the Apple Watch app on the iPhone and tap My Watch, then go to Photos and Synced Album and pick the album you want to sync; you can also create a new album using photos from your phone.

Storage

The watch does not have as much space as your phone so it's important to limit how much you store on it; to limit photo storage, open the Apple Watch app on the iPhone, tap My Watch, then go to Photos and Photo Limits.

You can see how many photos are currently on your Apple Watch by opening the Settings app from the watch's Home screen, tapping General, and then About. You can also see this on your phone by opening the Apple Watch app, then tapping My Watch, General, and About.

Camera Viewfinder

While the watch doesn't have a camera built in, it does have a pretty awesome feature that lets you use the watch as an external camera viewfinder and shutter to your iPhone camera.

For this to work, you need to make sure the watch is no more than 30 feet from your iPhone.

To take a photo, open the Camera app on your watches Home screen, then position the iPhone to frame the shot using the Apple Watch as your viewfinder. If you want to change the exposure, just tap the area you want to focus on from your Apple Watch preview; tap the shutter button on your watch. You can preview the photo on your watch, but the photo will actually be saved on the iPhone.

Next to the shutter button is a timer button; if you want to do a timed shot, tap that. The timer takes burst shots, which is great for action / sports photos.

Music

The Music app is, of course, on your Home screen, but you can reach it more quickly by swiping up on your screen.

Like almost anything on the watch, you can also play music with Siri. Just lift your wrist and say, "play Bob Dylan."

When music is playing, tap the top corner and you'll have the option to scroll through Artist, Albums, Playlist and Songs (scroll using the Digital Crown knob).

The watch automatically syncs to your phone and will play music that's on your iPhone. That's great when your phone is nearby, but sometimes you don't have your phone nearby and want to listen to music directly on your watch. You can load music to your watch pretty easily.

To add music, connect your watch to its charger, then open the Apple Watch app on your iPhone. Next, tap Music (it's near the bottom). After that, tap Sync Playlist, and choose the songs you want to add.

To play music directly from your watch, open the Music app and press firmly on the screen when the app opens. This will open a new menu with four options: Shuffle, Repeat, Source, and Airplay. Select Source. Next select Apple Watch. It will now walk you through pairing your watch with Bluetooth headsets to listen to the music.

From the previous menu, you can also select Airplay to pair your watch with an Airplay enabled speaker.

Stocks

If you'd like to monitor one or more stocks from your watch, open the Stocks app; you can see details about a stock by tapping it in the list and then turning the Digital Crown to scroll.

You can also use Siri to find a stock price by saying, "What was the closing price for XYZ stock?"

Weather

To open weather information, then go to the Weather app by opening it on the watch Home screen. The Weather app will have the 10-day forecast, current temperature and conditions, and chance of rain.

The Weather app is synced to your iPhone, so if you want to add or remove a city, then do it from your phone.

You can change the default city being shown on your watch by opening the Apple Watch app on your iPhone, tapping on My Watch, and then going to Weather and Default City.

Activity

One of the features that Apple is really promoting with the Apple Watch is Activity; one of the reasons to wear the watch, if you are to believe Apple, is to get you to move more. It's a hard sell with me, because I'm a lazy bum!

The app is divided up into three fitness goals: stand up for at least one minute of every hour, hit your calorie burn goal by moving more (you can set your goal), and accumulate 30 minutes of an activity that requires movement above a brisk walk. Each of these goals make up rings; as you complete your goals, the rings begin to fill up, and by the end of the day they should ideally be full.

To get started, go to your Home screen and tap the Activity app. The first time that you open the app, it will give you a very short tutorial on what the app is and how it helps you live a happier, healthier life. Once you finish the tutorial, you'll have to enter some personal information—this is for your eyes only and you only do it once. It will help ensure the app is as accurate as possible. For each section, turn the Digital Crown to enter your information.

After you've finished, you will indicate your activity level; you can change this later, so if you aren't sure, then go for lower—not higher. Next you'll see your suggested goal, which you can accept or adjust. When you are done, tap Start Moving. Your app will now be tracking you in the background. There's no need to start anything each day.

You can access the Activity app at any time by tapping on it from your Home screen. The first thing you'll see is all the rings together. You can use your Digital Crown to see more detailed information on the rings.

At any time, you can change your goals by opening the app, then pressing firmly on the display. You can also have reminders sent to you to encourage you to complete your goals.

In the Activity app on your iPhone, you can view your Activity history, and see more detailed reports about what you've done. The measurements will get more accurate as you wear the watch more and it gets to know your behaviors.

Finally, if you swipe left on the Activity app, you can share your activity goals; perfect for the lazy bum like me, who likes to remind his spouse that they were sitting around all day.

Most people, myself included, sit a little more than they care to admit. We sit at our job; we sit on our commute home from that job; and we sit when we get home. The problem with sitting is it's not great for our health.

Apple helps with a new Standing goal in WatchOS. With the new mode, you can set a goal for how long you want to stand.

The goal is to push you to stand more even when your job would otherwise have you sit; it will motivate you to take quick breaks and stand, which will help circulate your blood.

WORKOUT

Workout is kind of a companion to Activity even though there's a separate app for it. The point of it is to help you track progress during a workout session and help you hit new milestones.

From your Home screen, tap the Workout app and you'll immediately see dozens of different workouts. They range from brisk walks to more intense workouts—both indoor and outdoor. For indoor and outdoor running or walking and outdoor cycling, you can also set a distance goal. You can also choose no goal and simply get started.

The following are some of the workouts you can choose from:
- Outdoor walk
- Outdoor run
- Outdoor cycle
- Indoor walk
- Indoor run
- Indoor cycle
- Elliptical
- Rower
- Stair stepper
- High intensity interval training (HIIT)
- Hiking
- Yoga
- Functional strength training
- Dance
- Cooldown
- Core training
- Pool swim
- Open water swim

If you don't see what you are doing, tap Add Workout (no, this isn't where you track the fitness goal "watch TV"). This will also bring up options for the following sports: Badminton, Barre, Basketball, Cross Training, Kickboxing, Mixed Cardio, Pilates, Soccer, Social Dance, Surfing, Table Tennis, Tennis, Traditional Strength Training, American Football, Archery, Australian Football, Baseball, Bowling, Boxing, Climbing, Cricket, Cross Country Skiing, Cross Training, Curling, Disc Sports, Downhill Skiing, Equestrian Sports, Fencing, Fishing, Fitness

Gaming, Flexibility, Golf, Gymnastics, Hand Cycling, Handball, Hockey, Hunting, Jump Rope, Lacrosse, Martial Arts, Mind & Body, Paddling, Pickleball, Play, Rolling, Rugby, Sailing, Skating, Snow Sports, Snowboarding, Softball, Squash, Stairs, Step Training, Tai Chi, Track & Field, Volleyball, Water Fitness, Water Polo, and Wrestling—did they miss any sport?!

If you add any of those other sports by tapping it, then it will start showing up in the workouts, so you don't have to search for it again.

You can either start the workout or set goals. To set a goal (such as how far you want to walk), tap the three dots.

This will bring up four options: Open, Calories, Distance, and Time.

What these options will do is set a goal. So, as an example, let's say my goal is to walk three miles; I add three miles, then tap Begin, and it will start tracking. I'll get alerted when I hit three miles.

Once you hit Begin, the watch will immediately count down to start. During your workout, a ring will steadily fill in here as you approach your goal.

To pause or end the workout, just press firmly on the display and press End or Pause. When you end the workout, you can scroll through a full summary. You can either save the data or discard it. You might notice that some workouts have more options than others; that's because each workout has different configurations.

Fitness+

One of the biggest improvements coming to WatchOS is Fitness+; this is going to be a new Apple Service that is set to disrupt the fitness industry.

Apple provided a high-level overview of the service in September, but the actual service will not launch until later in the year.

It will cost $9.99 a month or $79.99 a year (with three months free if you buy a new Apple Watch); Fitness+ will also be bundled into the new Apple One Premier service ($29.99 / month), which gives you and your entire family access to all Apple Services.

The way the services will work is you pick the type of workout you want to do using either your Apple TV, iPad, or iPhone; this will sync up instantly with your watch. So while the video workout is playing, you'll see things like your heart rate on the video.

The workouts will change every week, and you can use them with or without exercise equipment. There are workouts for beginners and advanced users, and Apple's AI will recommend different workouts and trainers based on your workout regimen.

You can even filter the workouts by time (from five minutes to 45 minutes); so if you only have a few minutes in your schedule, you can find a workout routine that fits into that schedule.

If you have used (or are familiar with) Peloton, then it's a very similar concept. The biggest difference is it can work with more devices (or no device at all); that makes it great for traveling.

You'll also be able to choose the type of music that plays during your workout.

Check Your Heart Rate

To get the best results with your heart rate, make sure the watch is tight enough to touch the skin, but not too tight.

It will measure your heart rate when you load the app.

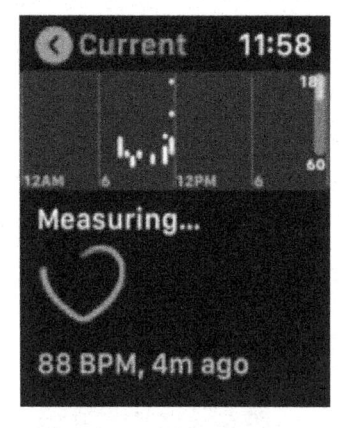

Tapping on any of the three options: Current, Resting Rate, or Walking Average, will get you an overview of your heart rate.

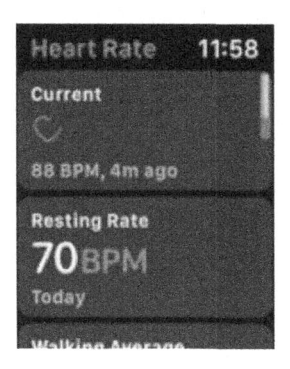

If you are in a workout, you can check your heart rate by swiping on the lower half of the Workout progress screen.

CYCLE TRACKING

Cycle Tracking isn't an app, rather it's a new feature in the Health app of your watch. It tracks your menstrual cycle and can help predict when your next period will come or when your fertile window is about to start. (Pay careful attention to that word "prediction"! The watch should obviously not be used as a form of birth control.)

To get started, put down your watch and open up your phone. Open the Health app, then go to Cycle Tracking and select Get Started.

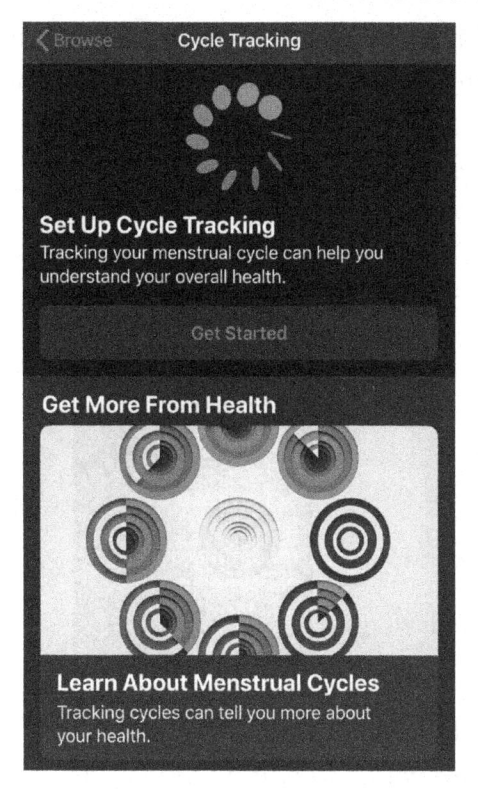

Follow the instructions and make sure and add the features you want (such as Period Prediction and Fertility Prediction).

Once your information is added, you can now start logging things like your flow level or other symptoms.

SLEEP TRACKING

Sleep tracking isn't entirely new to Apple; it was introduced to the iPhone some time ago; but the feature is new to Apple Watch. When you wear your watch at night, it can track how long you are sleeping (and waking in the middle of the night) and set goals to help you sleep better.

To get started, open the Sleep app on the watch.

The first time you use the app, you'll see a message about the app.

> **Sleep** 5:19
>
> **Set a Sleep Goal**
> Sleep can recommend a bedtime and wake-up alarm.

Scroll down a little, and you can set it up by first telling the watch how long you'd like to sleep for, and then scrolling just a tad further and tapping the Next button.

> **Sleep** 5:19
>
> ⊖ **8H 00M** ⊕
>
> After you wake up, Sleep can also let you know if you've hit your goal.

Next, it will ask when the schedule is active—only weekdays, for example.

Under this, you tell the device when you'd ideally like to wake up and toggle the button if you want an alarm.

Below this you set your bedtime; this will calculate your sleep and tell you if you can hit that goal. In the example below, for example, it says I will miss the goal by 1 hour and 15 minutes. So if I want to hit it, then I'll need to change my bedtime.

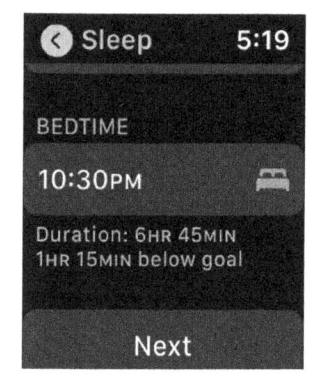

Once it's set up, you'll see a summary of the schedule, and you can scroll down to Enable it to turn on (hint: make sure and have your battery charged before bed if you are tracking sleep).

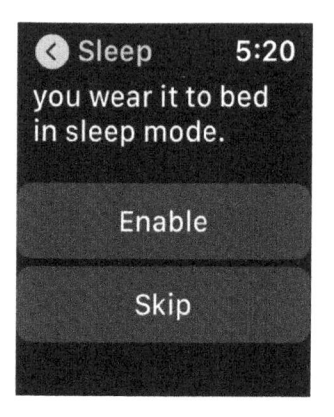

You can also set up a Wind Down schedule, which helps you relax before bed.

> **Sleep** 5:20
>
> **Wind Down**
> Sleep mode can begin before bedtime to reduce distractions and help you relax. This

Finally, you can turn on charge reminders, which will remind you before bed to charge your device, so you have enough power to get through the night.

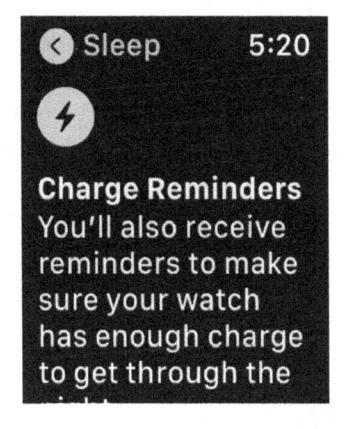

> **Sleep** 5:20
>
> **Charge Reminders**
> You'll also receive reminders to make sure your watch has enough charge to get through the

You can edit the schedule at any time. Just tap the schedule and tap the time you want to change.

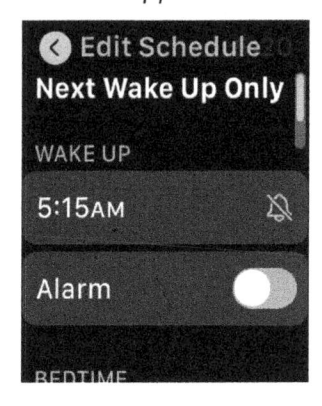

Set Alarms

If you want to set an alarm, go to the Alarm Clock app from your watch's Home screen.

Once it's open, press firmly on the display, then tap Add Alarm. Tap Change Time (remember to also change AM / PM); you can use the Digital Crown knob to adjust the hours and minutes. Finally tap Set. You can tap the '<' in the upper left corner to return to the alarm settings, where you can repeat an alarm, push snooze, or label it.

To adjust an alarm, tap the Alarm Clock app, then tap the alarm in the list that you want to change. Tap next to the alarm to turn it on or off. You can delete an alarm by tapping on the alarm, then scrolling to the bottom and tapping Delete.

Once you've used the watch for sleep tracking, you'll begin seeing the results in the Health app on your iPhone.

From the Health app, go to the Browse tab, and then select the Sleep option.

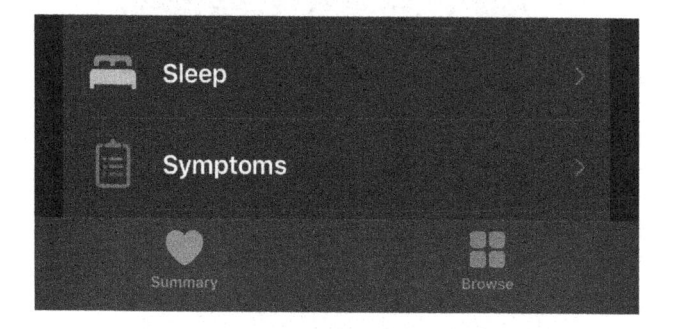

You'll see a chart of how you slept; blue is sleep, and gaps would be wake periods.

If you scroll a little further down, you'll see your heart rate while you slept.

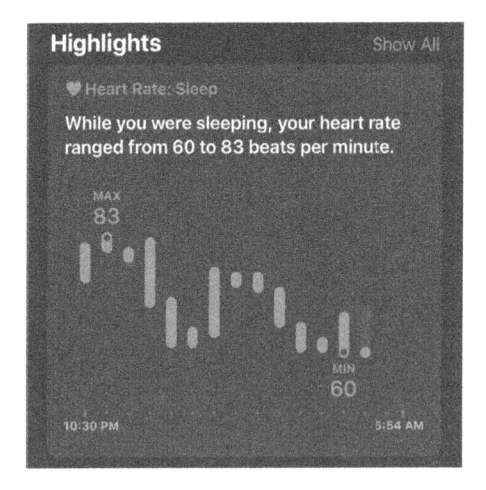

If you go all the way to the bottom, you'll see an option to Show All Data.

This can give you even more insight about how you slept; you may not even realize how much you toss and turn.

USE A TIMER

To use the watch's timer, go to the Home screen and tap Timer; timers can be set for up to 24 hours. To set a timer, open the app, tap hours or minutes, turn the Digital Crown knob to adjust the time, and finally tap Start. If the timer will be more than 12 hours, then while adjusting the timer press firmly on the display and tap 0-24 hours.

Use the Stopwatch

If you want to use the stopwatch to time things like the time of a track lap, then go to your Home screen and tap the Stopwatch app. To start the watch, tap the Start button; tap the Lap button to split the time or record a lap. Timing will continue as you switch between them. When you are finished, tap Reset.

You can also pick the format for the stopwatch. There are four different ones: Analog, Digital, Graph, and Hybrid.

Audiobooks

Apple has not yet put their popular Books app on the Apple Watch—probably because reading is just not a great experience on the watch. There are third-party apps that do this if it's a must-have feature. What Apple offers in the place of a native bookstore is the ability to listen to audiobooks that you purchased from the Apple Books store.

It's a pretty straightforward app; scroll to the audiobook that you want and tap it.

From here, you can play the book, or fast-forward / rewind. The '1x' in the lower right corner adjusts the playback speed, so you can have the narrator read faster.

Calculator

Simple calculations could be performed on the watch by using Siri in earlier versions of the Apple Watch, but a native app was missing. Many people are surprised it took so long to get this app on the watch. Whatever the reason for the wait, it's here now, and it does more than you might expect.

In addition to basic calculations there's a Tip button. This helps you quickly see how much of a tip you should leave. Type in the cost, then tap the Tip button. You can use the Digital Crown to adjust the percentage.

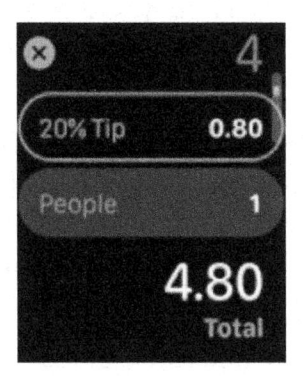

Tap the People button below the percentage and you can split the bill. Use the Digital Crown to adjust how many people are with you. As you add people, it will show the cost for each person below the final price.

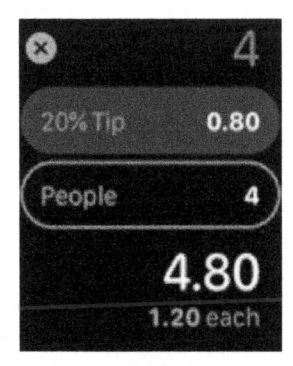

Handwashing

Okay, let's first talk about the elephant in the room: do we really need an app to tell us how to wash our hands? Wash, soap, rinse, right?

It sounds silly, but the terrifying thing is how improperly most of us do it. Go ahead...try the app and see if you actually wash for the full 20 seconds consistently. According to Apple, who did a study on this, as many as 95% of us don't do it right. Yikes, right? So next time you shake someone's hand, look at their wrist to see if they have an Apple Watch to help them do it right!

If you are Mr. Clean and don't need an app to tell you how perfect you are, just turn it off—and if you are a Mr. Dirty, and don't need an app to remind you, then you can turn it off as well.

So how does it work? The beauty of the app is it works with no effort on your part. Once you turn it on, it will automatically detect you are washing your hands and start the timer.

To turn it on go to the Settings app, and then scroll until you see Handwashing.

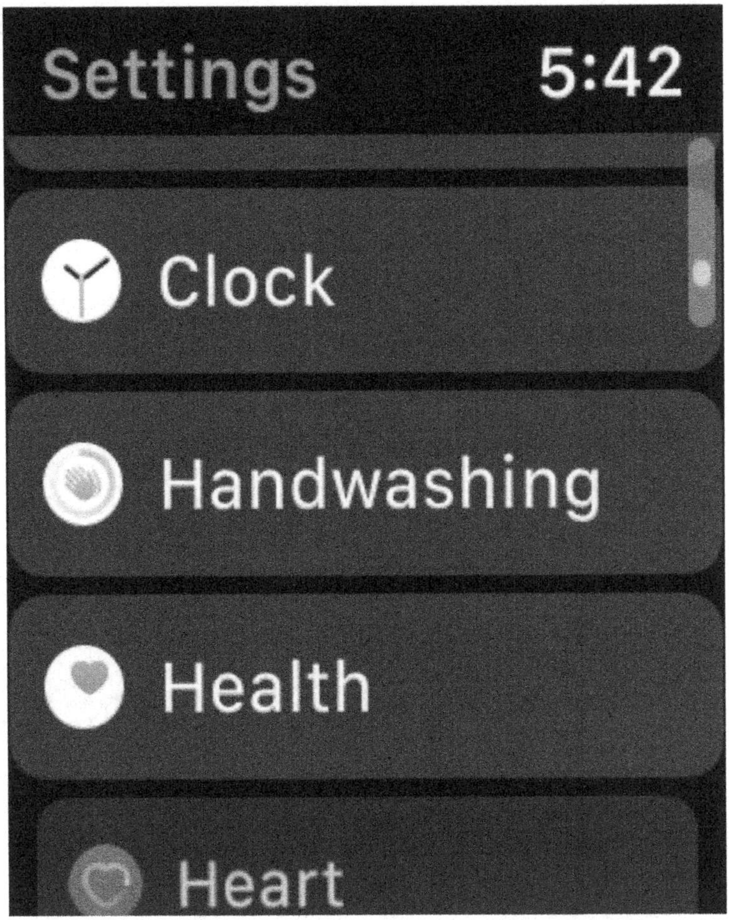
Settings
5:42
Clock
Handwashing
Health
Heart

Tap it, and then toggle the timer to on (it will be green). That's it. Test it by washing your hands.

If you don't see the timer right away, give it a couple of seconds. It's both listening for water and detecting the motion of you washing your hands. Once the timer starts, you'll see a notification on your wrist and the timer will stay on the screen until it's done.

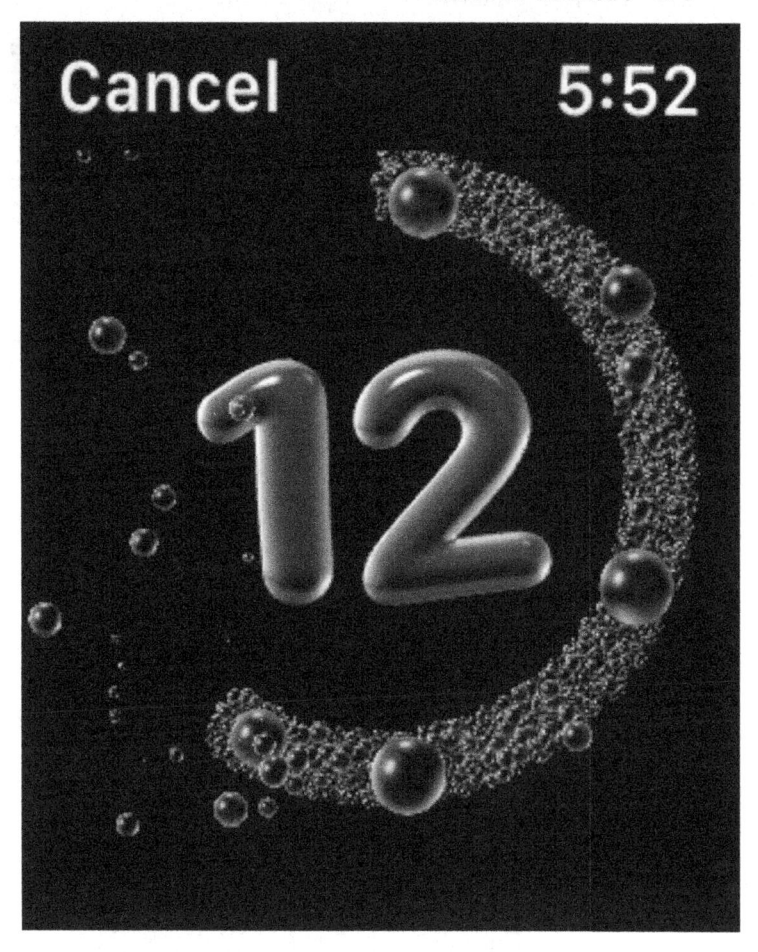

That's great, but how do you get the stats about how unclean you are?! You'll need your iPhone for that.

Go to the Health app; on the bottom of the screen are two tabs: Summary and Browse.

The washing app is under Browse. You can do one of two things to find it: search for it or go to Other.

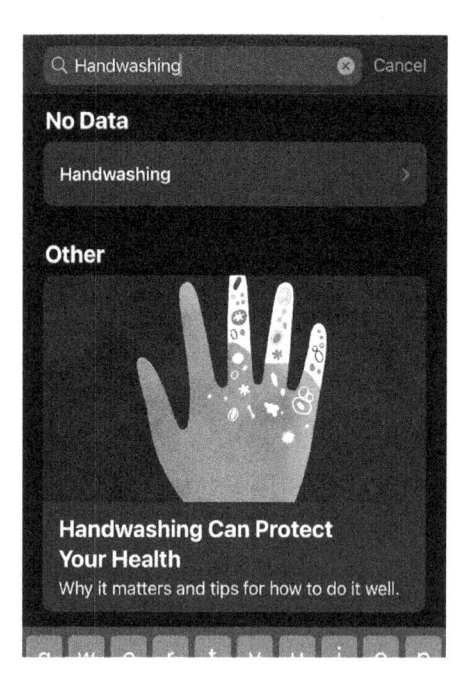

This is going to bring up all the available data the app has on your washing habits. In my case, none! I swear I've been washing my hands! The below is just an early screen grab.

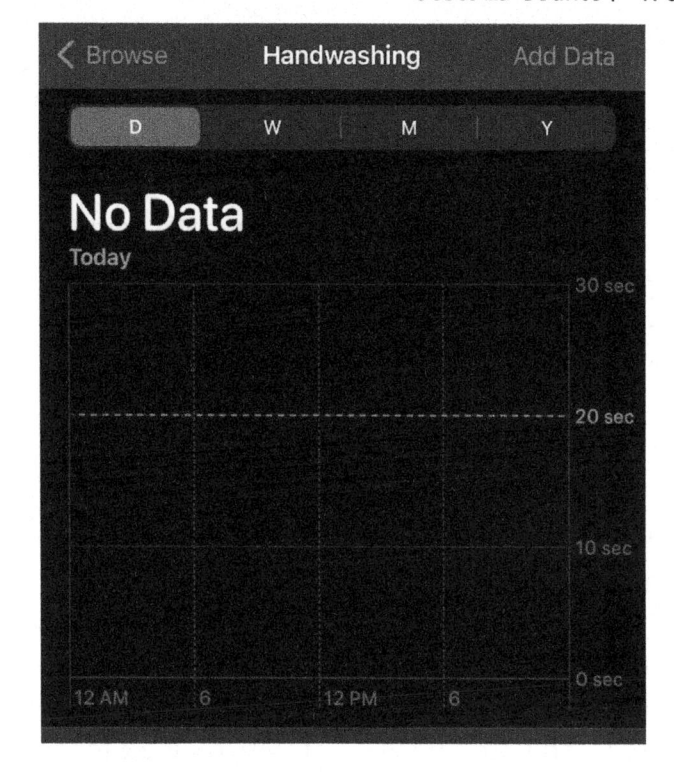

If I really wanted to, I could go to Add Data and manually add in my handwashing times.

Remote Control

A lesser-known fact about the watch is that it doubles as a remote control for iTunes and Apple TV.

Before you begin, make sure both your watch and your device are using the same network; if your phone is using one Wi-Fi and your watch is using another, then they won't work.

Remote Play iTunes

If you'd like to use the watch as a remote for iTunes on your Mac, open up the Remote app; next tap the Add Device (+).

In iTunes on your computer, click the Remote button near the top of the iTunes window; it will ask you to enter the 4-digit code that is now displayed on your watch. (Note: if you look for the Remote button in iTunes before you tap Add Device on the Apple Watch, you'll be waiting a long time—it will only appear after you tap Add Device; also make sure iTunes is up-to-date.)

Remote for Apple TV

If you'd like to use the watch as a remote for iTunes on your Apple TV, open up the Remote app; next tap the Add Device (+). (Note: remember you must be using the same Wi-Fi Network.)

On your Apple TV go to Settings, and then General, and finally Remote, and select the Apple Watch; enter the passcode that's currently on your watch.

WALKIE-TALKIE

WatchOS 5 made it a whole lot easier to communicate with those close by with its Walkie-Talkie feature. WatchOS 7 keeps this feature. To use it, both people need to have an Apple Watch Series 1 or later and WatchOS 7. You also need to turn on FaceTime because you will be using FaceTime Audio.

Unfortunately, this feature is not available in all countries.

The first time you use the app, you will need to add friends. Open the app. Tap ⊕, then choose a contact.

Now wait. It's not like a phone call where it connects right away with your friend. They have to give you permission to reach them. It will stay gray until the person accepts. Once they accept you can start talking away instantly.

To remove a friend, open the Walkie-Talkie app, swipe left on the friend, then tap ✕. Or open the Apple Watch app on your iPhone, tap Walkie-Talkie > Edit, tap ⊖, then tap Remove.

To start a conversation, just open the app, tap the friend's name (after they've accepted), and wait for it to connect (they have to be wearing the watch). Once connected, tap Talk and say something, then let go when you are done.

You can turn the volume up and down with the Digital Crown.

If you no longer want to talk over this feature, just open it and toggle it to off; if a contact tries to reach you, it will say you are unavailable.

If you turn on Silent mode, you can still hear the person's voice and the chimes that come in. If you turn on Theater mode or Do Not Disturb then it will make you unavailable to talk.

Family Setup

If you have a child and want to keep them safe and connected, but don't want to let them have a phone yet, Apple Watch is now a viable option for many families.

Family Setup allows children to have a phone number, but on a device that doesn't have an Internet browser and other apps that you might feel uncomfortable with them having.

It also allows you to control who they call and what exactly they can do.

The catch (aside from having to buy another watch) is it only works with Apple Watch Series 4 or later, and it needs a cellular plan to take advantage of all the features.

To set it up, you'll get started just like you would any Apple Watch; if you are using an old Apple Watch for this, then you need to factory reset it.

When you turn on Apple Watch to pair the watch, you'll want to select Set Up for a Family Member.

178 | *Getting Started With Apple Watch SE*

Next, you see a box about what Family Setup is.

Once you agree to the terms and pair the watch, it will ask you to pick the family member using the device. If you don't see them, then tap Add New Family Member.

Choose Family Member

Select the family member who will be using this Apple Watch.

Add New Family Member...

If you are adding someone new, there will be a number of steps you need to complete. They'll just be questions about what you are sharing and what will be enabled.

Family Member's Apple ID

If this person already has an Apple ID, they can use it to sign in to this Apple Watch.

Family Sharing will be set up for you and your family member so you can share location, purchases, and more. You will become the family organizer, and this person will join your family.

Your family will also get the ability to help locate each others' devices.

Your Apple ID information is used to enable Apple services when you sign in, including iCloud Backup which automatically backs up the data on your device in case you need to replace or restore it. Your device serial number may be used to check eligibility for service offers. See how your data is managed.

Use Existing Apple ID

Create New Apple ID

One pretty cool feature to Family Setup is Apple Cash Family; this lets you share Apple Pay with that family member; so you can give them access to $20 that they can use for food or anything else; it works like Apple Pay on the phone—they tap their watch to a card reader that accepts it and the money is taken.

The last thing it will ask you about is turning on Schooltime; I cover Schooltime in the next section, but if you want to set up a schedule, then this is where you can do it at.

SCHOOLTIME

If you have Family Setup on a child's device, then you can use Schooltime to create schedules—so, for example, you can say from 9 to 3 turn Schooltime on; during this time, the watch will be limited with features, so a child can't play games while they're supposed to be studying.

The child can briefly exit Schooltime mode to check things like messages, by turning the Digital Crown and confirming they want to exit. It will automatically turn back on when they're done. You'll also be able to see a full history of when they turned it off and for how long.

Schooltime is compatible with Apple Watch Series 4 and up (and the Apple Watch SE), so if you want to give an older watch to your child while you get a new one, then just make sure it's a 4 and up—to get the most of its features, then you also want to have the cellular model. If you only have the Wi-Fi model, you "technically" can still use it, but it will lack most of the core features—notably a phone number for the device.

If you decide to give your child an older watch for Family Setup, then you need to do a factory reset on it and set it up as a new device.

To setup a Schooltime schedule, open the Watch app on your iPhone, then tap your child's watch; if you don't see it, then you probably haven't set up Family Setup yet, so refer to that section to learn how. Next tap Schooltime, then select Edit Schedule. From here you can pick the days and times that you want it to be active for—you can also add breaks, so if you want them to have full access to their watch during recess, then you can edit it here. If you need to change the schedule, then follow the steps above, but tap the information button next to the managed watch, and tap Schooltime and Edit Schedule.

If you have not done a Family Setup for the device, but still like the idea of the mode, you can manually turn it on by swiping up and tapping the little guy raising his hand. You turn it off the same way.

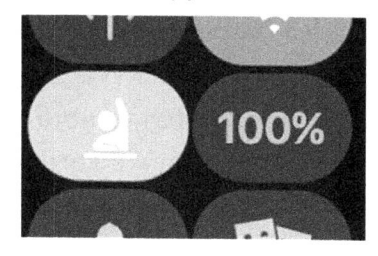

To use Schooltime on your own Apple Watch, you need WatchOS 7 or later.

[8]
What Other Things Should I Know About the Apple Watch?

This chapter will cover:
- Accessibility features
- How to care for the Apple Watch
- How to reset the Apple Watch
- How to update the Apple Watch

Like every Apple product, the Apple Watch has accessibility features to help people with disabilities.

It works very similarly to your iPhone; to access the features, go to the Apple Watch app on your iPhone, then My Watch, then General, and finally Accessibility.

VOICEOVER

VoiceOver helps you use the watch even if you can't see the watch. It will read back everything that's on the watch for you. You can turn it on by going to the Settings app on the watch's Home screen, then General, Accessibility, and finally VoiceOver.

When VoiceOver is on, you can move your finger around the display and listen to the name of each item you touch. VoiceOver also uses different gestures; you can go back by using two fingers to draw a "Z" shape on the display. To open an app, you will double tap it instead of single tap. To pause the VoiceOver from reading what's on the screen, tap the display with two fingers; tap with two fingers again to resume play.

When you set up your watch for the first time, you can use VoiceOver as well. When you turn on the watch for the first time, press the side button; after it turns on, triple click the Digital Crown knob.

ZOOM

The watch is a small display—perhaps even smaller than you thought it would be—so it's understandable that you might want the display a little bigger. If that's the case, go to the Settings app, and then turn on General, Accessibility, and Zoom.

To zoom in or out when Zoom is enabled you will double tap the display with two fingers. To move around (or pan) the display, you will drag with two fingers.

Bold Text

Putting the text in boldface is another way to make reading the text on your screen a little easier. You can make the text boldface by going to the Settings app on your Home screen, then tapping General and Accessibility and turning on Bold Text; the watch will need to be restarted before this goes into effect.

Handling

Removing the Bands

To change a band, press the band release button on the Apple Watch and slide the band across, then slide in the new band. You should never force a band into the slot, as this could get it stuck.

It is recommended that you fit the band so it is close to your skin, but not so tight that it is squeezing your wrist.

Band Care

Apple recommends that you clean the leather portions of bands with a nonabrasive, lint-free cloth that is, if necessary, dampened with water. The band should not be attached to the watch while cleaning. After cleaning, let the band dry before re-attaching to the watch. Do not store leather in direct sunlight, or in high temperatures or high humidity; you also should not soak the leather in water as it is not water resistant.

For all other bands, Apple recommends cleaning the same way, but the band should be dried with a nonabrasive, lint-free cloth.

A Little More Advanced

Force Restarting the Apple Watch

In very rare cases, the Apple Watch may freeze or need to be force restarted. If this ever happens, hold down the side button and Digital Crown knob at the same time for ten seconds. When the Apple logo appears, you can let go.

Resetting the Watch Settings

If you want to reset the watch settings and make the watch like new (remember this erases everything), then go to the Settings app from the Home screen, then go to General, Reset, and finally

Erase All Content and Settings. Once it's reset you will need to pair it with your phone again. Make sure you do this if you ever sell or give your watch or phone away, as your vital information (like credit cards) will be available to that person if you don't.

GET YOUR WATCH DNA

If you need to know what model number your watch is, what software version it is, what its serial number is, or what its capacity is then go to the Settings app from your Home screen, and then General and About.

UPDATE APPLE WATCH SOFTWARE

Much like the iPhone and iPad, updates to the Apple Watch software are done over the air—meaning you won't need to plug anything in.

To see if there's an update, open the Apple Watch app on the iPhone, then tap My Watch, General, and finally Software Updates. It will tell you if there's an update, and then you just follow the steps. Updates don't happen very often—usually just a handful of times each year.

[9]
So Many Bands and Accessories, So Little Time

> This chapter will cover:
> - Official Apple Watch bands and accessories

Watch Bands & Accessories

What's a watch without its band? Unlike traditional bands, the Apple Watch makes it remarkably easy to switch out bands. And unlike any other Apple product, you have lots of options; normally an Apple product comes in two or three colors, but with the watches there are several dozen ways to mix and match.

Below is a guide to all the different options you have to choose from. (Note: when purchasing a band, remember that a 42mm band won't be compatible with a 38mm watch or vice versa.) Unless otherwise noted, all bands are available in both 38 and 42mm. Some bands are not one size fits all.

Official Bands & Accessories

Solo Loop

Some people aren't fans of watch buckles; if that sounds like you, then the Solo Loop might make a good fit. It's made of a stretchable rubber, so it just slips on. It comes in several sizes and you'll want to take measurements before buying to make sure you get the best fit.

BRAIDED SOLO LOOP

The Braided Solo Loop is similar to the Solo Loop, but it has an interwoven look. It also slips over your wrist, so there are no buckles.

SPORT BAND

It's available in black, space gray, white, pink, blue, and green. The band is obviously best for working out; it's also the cheapest band available. It's made of fluoroelastomer, a synthetic rubber known for performing well in heat. Because this band isn't one size fits all, the chart below helps you make the right choice:

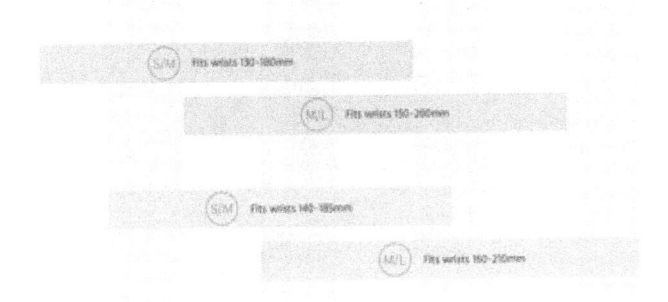

- (S/M) Fits wrists 130-180mm
- (M/L) Fits wrists 150-200mm
- (S/M) Fits wrists 140-185mm
- (M/L) Fits wrists 160-210mm

CLASSIC BUCKLE

This band is made of Dutch leather from a tannery in the Netherlands. Apple promises the mill gives it a distinctive texture. The closer is made of stainless steel.

Milanese Loop

Apple says the inspiration for this stainless-steel mesh band was a mesh band from 19th century Milan. The band is completely magnetic and easy to put on.

Modern Buckle

Three sizes: small, medium, and large.

It's available in brown, black, pink, and midnight blue. The leather for this stunning band comes from a French tannery established in 1803. How are the modern and classic bands different? The leather is slightly different, but the most noticeable difference is the buckle. The classic is a strap with holes; the modern is a magnetic band that helps you have a more precise fit. Because this band isn't one size fits all, the chart below helps you make the right choice:

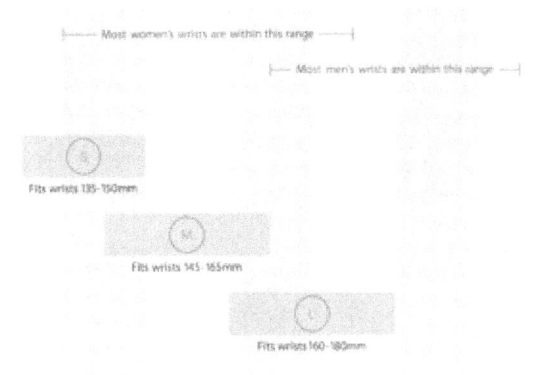

|—— Most women's wrists are within this range ——|

|—— Most men's wrists are within this range ——|

S
Fits wrists 135-150mm

M
Fits wrists 145-165mm

L
Fits wrists 160-180mm

LINK BRACELET

One of the most expensive and complex bands, this stainless-steel band has over 100 parts. Apple claims the craftsmanship is so complex that it takes nine hours to assemble a single case. The magnetic closure is one size fits all.

Leather Loop

Only available for the 42mm band.

It's available in stone, light brown, bright blue, and black. Made of Venezia leather and hand-crafted in Arzignano, Italy, this band has a soft and gilded feel. The magnetic loop is easy to put on. Because this band isn't one size fits all, the chart below helps you make the right choice:

M   Fits wrists 150-185mm

L   Fits wrists 180-210mm

APPLE WATCH MAGNETIC CHARGING CABLE

($29 for 1m cable; $39 for 2m cable)

Apple has only announced one official accessory for the Apple Watch, and that is an extra charger (one comes free with your watch).

[10]
Apple Cares?

This chapter will cover:
- What's covered under the standard Apple Watch warranty?
- What's AppleCare?

Warranty

Because of how delicate the watch can be it's important to understand what's covered and what's not covered under the watch warranty.

Covered

Debris under the display glass or pixel anomaly; the back cover is removed but there is no damage (by damage, there should be absolutely no evidence that the cover was removed by prying); and finally, condensation in the heart rate sensor windows.

COVERED WITH FEES

Damages that are covered out-of-warranty include cracked, missing, removed, or damaged Digital Crown cap; abrasions, puncture holes, missing buttons from a drop, chips in the display, a removed back cover with damage, a bent band enclosure, a missing band release, or any cracks on the back cover.

Fees do apply to these services, and the cost depends on the model and if you have AppleCare+.

INELIGIBLE FOR SERVICE

The following damages are considered ineligible for warranty services: disassembled unit or missing parts, catastrophic damage, counterfeit or third-party parts, and lastly unauthorized modifications. (Note: catastrophic damage may be covered with AppleCare+; check with the Apple Store and explain the situation; it's provided at their discretion.)

AppleCare

Every Apple Watch does come with AppleCare; for extended service, however, AppleCare also offers AppleCare+.

What's the difference? The free level care includes a one year limited warranty for hardware repairs and 90 days of free technical support. AppleCare+ extends the warranty for two years. For the pricier Apple Watch Edition, this warranty is extended an additional year. With AppleCare+ you get two incidences of accidental damage (fees do apply).

Before paying for AppleCare+, one thing you should consider doing is checking the services your credit card offers; some credit cards will offer warranty extensions if you use their card for purchase. Some even consider loss or theft (which, by the way, AppleCare+ does not cover).

So, is AppleCare+ worth it? Personally, I like it for peace of mind; I don't have to worry about expensive cases or banging the watch on something. Apple Stores have terrific customer support when it comes to AppleCare+.

As companies learn about what makes the watch tick, services are bound to pop up that offer repairs more cheaply than what AppleCare+ charges; but Apple will always be the simplest way to repair your watch.

[11]
Apple Music

Apple Music is Apple's music streaming service. This chapter is included as a bonus supplement to help you control Apple Music on your iPhone.

The question most people wonder is which is better: Spotify or Apple Music? On paper it's hard to tell. They both have the same number of songs, and they both cost the same ($9.99 a month, $5 for students, $14.99 for families).

There really is no clear winner. It all comes down to preference. Spotify has some good features—such as an ad-supported free plan.

One of the standout features of Apple Music is iTunes Match. If you are like me and have a large collection of audio files on your computer, then you'll love iTunes Match. Apple puts those files in the cloud, and you can stream them on any of your devices. This feature is also available if you don't have Apple Music for $25 a year.

Apple Music also plays well with Apple devices; so, if you are an Apple house (i.e. everything you own, from smart speakers to TV media boxes, has the Apple logo), then Apple Music is probably the best one for you.

Apple is compatible with other smart speakers, but it's built to shine on its own devices.

I won't cover Spotify here, but my advice is to try them both (they both have free trials) and see which interface you prefer.

Apple Music Crash Course

Before going over where things are in Apple Music, it's worth noting that Apple Music can now be accessed from your web browser (in beta form) here: http://beta.music.apple.com.

It's also worth noting that I have a little girl and don't get to listen to a lot of "adult" music, so the examples here are going to show a lot of kids music!

The main navigation on Apple Music is at the bottom. There are five basic menus to select from:
- Library
- For You
- Browse
- Radio
- Search

Library

When you create playlists or download songs or albums, this is where you will go to find them.

You can change the categories that show up in this first list by tapping on Edit, then checking off the categories you want. Make sure to hit Done to save your changes.

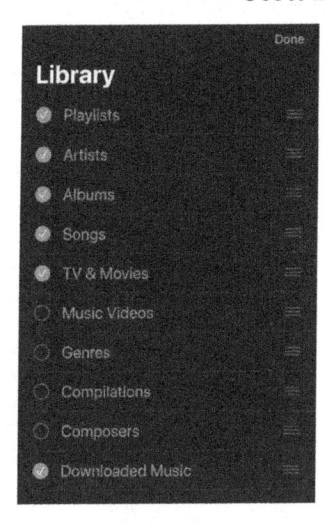

When you tap on the playlist you want to play, you can also share it with your friends by tapping on the three dots that show the options menu, and then tapping on Share Playlist.

For You

As you play music, Apple Music starts to get to know you more and more; it makes recommendations based on what you are playing. In For You, you can get a mix of all these songs and see other recommendations.

In addition to different styles of music, it also has friends' recommendations so you can discover new music based on what your friends are listening to.

Browse

Not digging those recommendations? You can also browse genres in the Browse menu. In addition to different genre categories, you can see what music is new and what music is popular.

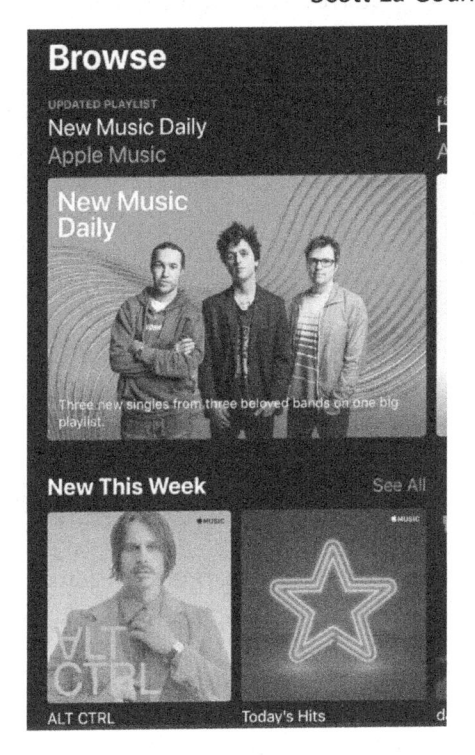

Radio

Radio is Apple's version of AM/FM; the main radio station is Beats One. There are on-air DJs and everything you'd expect from a radio station.

While Beats One is Apple's flagship station, it's not its only station. You can scroll down and tap on Radio Stations under More to explore and see several other stations based on music styles (i.e. country, alternative, rock, etc.). Under this menu, you'll also find a handful of talk stations covering news and sports. Don't expect to find the opinionated talk radio you may listen to on regular radio—it's pretty controversy-free.

Search

The last option is the search menu, which is pretty self-explanatory. Type in what you want to find (i.e. artist, album, genre, etc.).

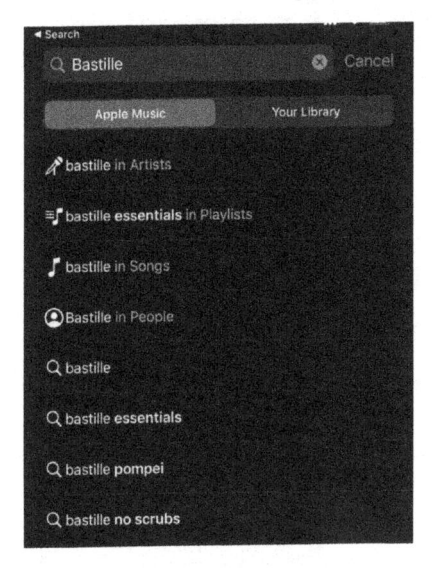

Listening to Music and Creating a Playlist

You can access the music you are currently listening to from the bottom of your screen.

This brings up a full screen of what you are listening to with several options.

The play, back/forward, and volume buttons are pretty straightforward. The buttons below that might look new.

The first option is for lyrics. If the song is paused, then you can read through the lyrics; if the song is playing, then it will bold the lyrics to the song it is currently playing. If you ever caught yourself wondering if the singer is saying "dense" or "dance" then this feature is a gamechanger.

The middle option lets you pick where you play the music. For example, if you have a HomePod and you want to listen wirelessly to the music from that device, you can change it here.

The last option shows the next song(s) in the playlist.

If you want to add a song to a playlist, then click the three dots next to the album/artist name. This brings up a list of several options (you can also go here to love or hate a song—which helps Apple Music figure out what you like); the option you want is Add to a Playlist. If you don't have a playlist or want to add it to a new one, then you can also create one here.

Scott La Counte | 213

City of Black & White	
Mat Kearney	
Copy	📋
Share Song...	📤
View Album	>
Add to Library	+
Add to a Playlist...	≡
View Full Lyrics	💬
Create Station	📡
Love	♡
Suggest Less Like This	👎

At any point, you can tap the artist's name to see all of their music.

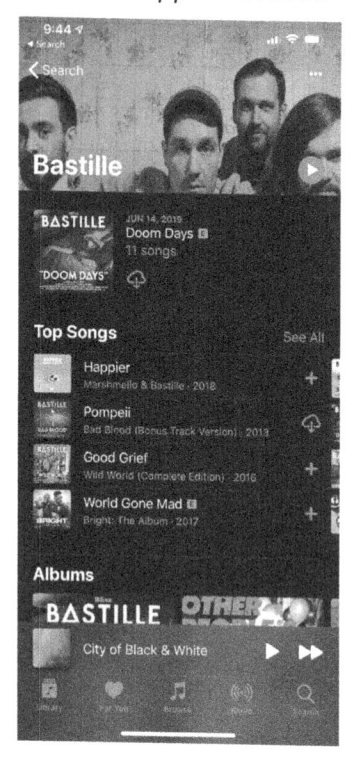

In addition to seeing information about the band, their popular songs, and their albums, you can get a playlist of their essential songs or a playlist of bands that they have influenced.

If you scroll to the bottom, you can also see Similar Artists, which is a great way to discover new bands that are like the ones you are currently listening to.

Tips for Getting the Most Out of Apple Music

Heart It

Like what your hearing? Heart it! Hate it? Dislike it. Apple gets to know you by what you listen to, but it improves the accuracy when you tell it what you think of a song you are really into…or really hate.

Use Settings

Some of the most resourceful features of Apple Music aren't in Apple Music—they're in your settings.

Open the Settings app, and scroll down to Music.

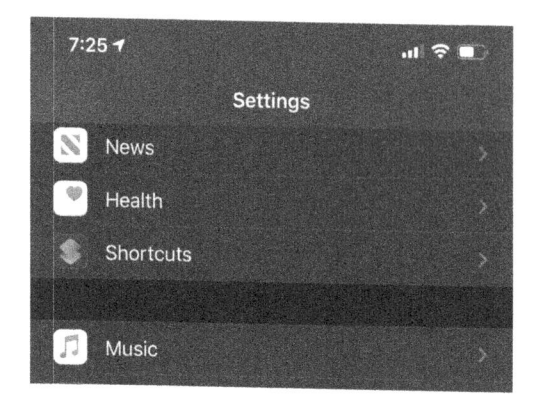

There are a few things to note here.

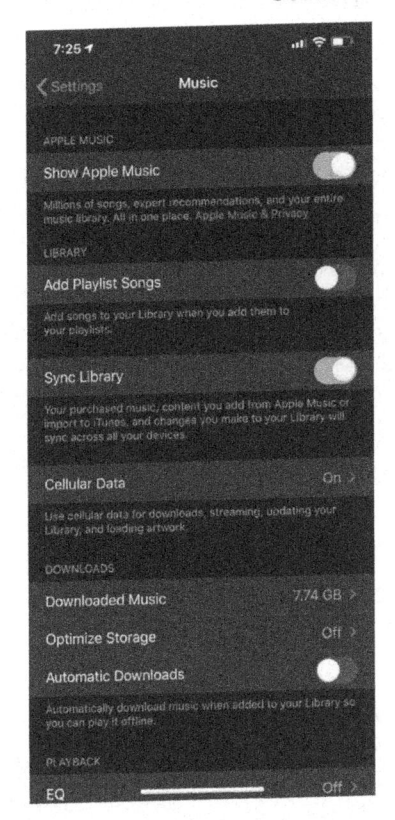

The first is under Cellular Data. Tap that and you'll see an option to turn high quality streaming on and off. If you want the best quality even when you are using data, then turn it on.

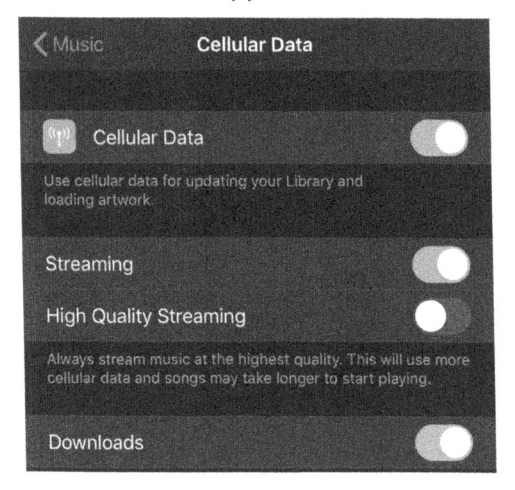

Next, go to Optimize Storage. If you are running short on space, then make sure and tap to toggle off.

Want to change the way your music sounds—such as more or less bass—go to EQ in the settings.

Download Music

If you don't want to rely on data when you are on the go, make sure and tap the Cloud on your music to download the music locally to your phone. If you don't see a cloud, add it to your library by tapping the plus, which should change it to a cloud.

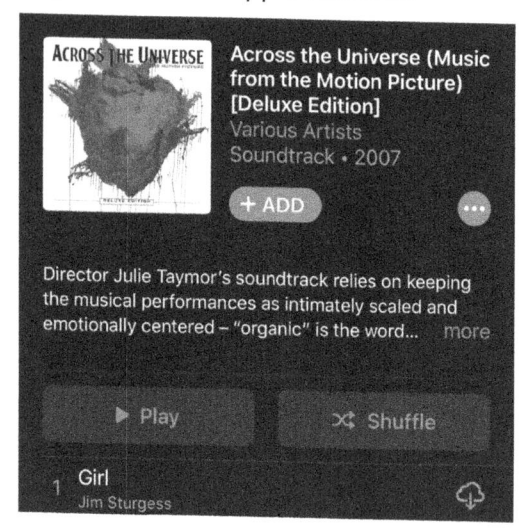

Hey Siri

Siri knows music! Say "Hey Siri" and say what you want to listen to, and the AI will get to work.

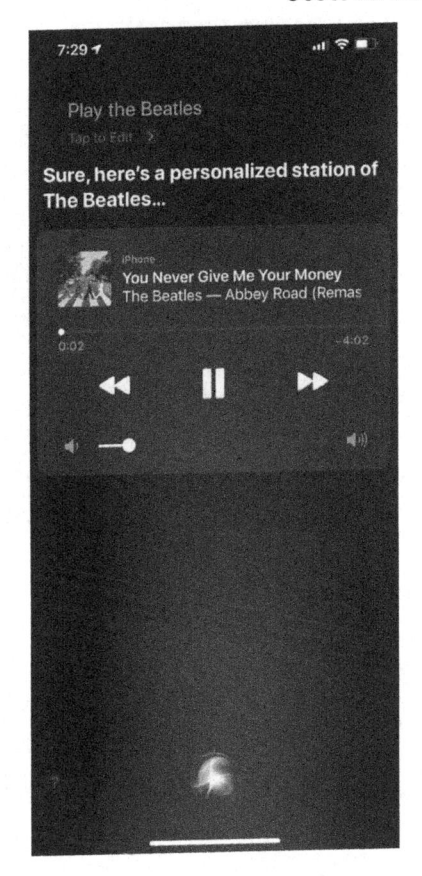

Wake Up to Music

If you'd like to wake up to a song instead of a buzzing noise, open your alarm. Next, tap "Sound."

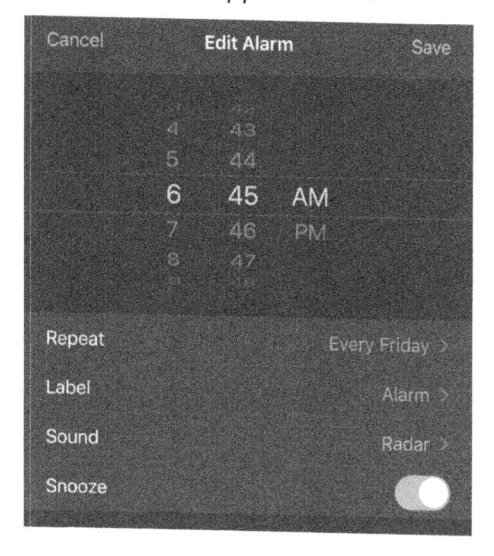

From here, select "Pick a Song."

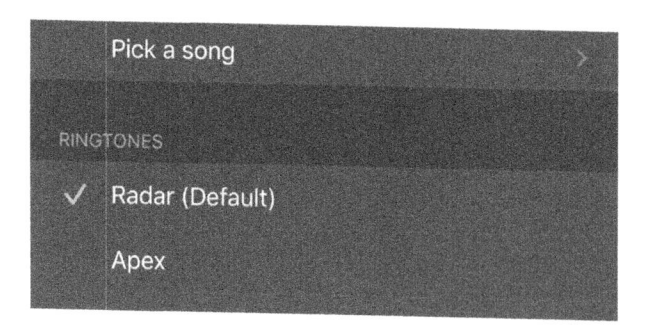

Finally, pick your music.

Library

- Playlists
- Artists
- Albums
- Songs
- Music Videos
- Genres
- Compilations
- Composers
- Downloaded Music

Appendix: The Apps

Apple Apps

This book has covered all the important apps already on the watch, but for a quick overview, here they are again.

- Messages - This is where you will send and receive text messages (and also send and receive animated emojis).
- Phone - This is, obviously, where you make and receive calls, but it should be noted that when you are using the phone on your wrist, you can also transfer that call to your iPhone, so if you step into a place where speakerphone is frowned upon, you don't have to hang up and call back.
- Mail - You can read your mail, but it's not for replying—it's more for managing mail (i.e., deleting, reading, flagging, and moving).

- Calendar – This app lets you quickly browse through your calendar and also accept and decline invitations.
- Activity – This app is a bit of a motivational workout app—it gives you a summary of how much you are standing, exercising, moving...in short it makes you feel guilty about how lazy you are.
- Workout – When you are working out, you tell your watch what you are doing (running, walking, cycling) and then it shows you how far you've gone, and how fast you are going.
- Maps – A turn-by-turn map...with a twist—when it's time for you to turn, it taps you on the wrist.
- Passbook – This is essentially a micro version of Passbook for the iPhone, but instead of holding your phone to the scanner, you hold your wrist.
- Siri – Siri is one of the most important apps on the Apple Watch because with no keyboard, you need it to find things quickly; to use it, just lift your wrist and start talking—no buttons need to be pressed.
- Music – The Music app is what you'd expect...unless you expect to plug in headsets; there's no audio input on the watch so you have to use Bluetooth headphones to listen.
- Camera Remote – The watch has no built-in camera; what it has in its place is a viewfinder, so if you want to take a selfie with

your phone, then you can use the watch to take the photo.
- Remote – If you have an Apple TV, this app lets you control it from your wrist; you can also use it to control your Mac or PC's iTunes library.
- Weather – Lets you see a visual summary of weather where you are or anywhere else in the world.
- Stocks – With this app you can see stock performance for up to six months.
- Photos – This is where you will view all your favorite photos.
- Alarm / Stopwatch / Timer – These are three relatively simple apps that do exactly what you'd expect them to do.
- World Clock – While the watch's time face screen is the main feature, it does have a second app for tracking time around the world.
- Settings – This is where you can turn off Wi-Fi, Bluetooth, etc.

INDEX

A

Accessibility 185, 186, 187
Activity .41, 79, 144, 145, 146, 147, 225
Activity Analog 79
Airplane Mode 52, 58, 62
Alarms 160
App Store 16, 17, 70, 105
Apple Care 199
Apple Music 12, 142, 202, 203, 205, 209, 212, 215, 216, 219, 221, 225
Apple Pay 12, 28, 64, 127, 180
Apps 67, 69, 224
Audiobooks 165

B

Band Car 188
Battery 45, 47, 48, 49
Battery Health.............. 47, 49
Bluetooth 27, 52, 143, 225, 226
Breathe 12, 75, 82
Brightness 43

C

Calculator....................... 166
Calendar.....12, 132, 134, 135, 225
Camera.................... 141, 225

Cellular

Cellular 217
Charging 45, 48, 49, 197
Compass 75
Compass App 75
Control Center 57
Cycle Tracking 153, 154

D

Digital Crown... 43, 44, 49, 55, 61, 63, 70, 75, 78, 83, 93, 97, 98, 103, 128, 130, 131, 135, 136, 139, 140, 142, 143, 145, 146, 160, 163, 167, 176, 182, 186, 188, 200
Do Not Disturb 18, 52, 177

E

ECG................................ 22
Elliptical.......................... 148
Email 127, 128, 129
Emoji 119
Events............................ 134

F

FaceTime 25, 175
Find My 62
Fitness+ 17, 150, 151
Force Restarting 188
Force Touch...... 39, 55, 60, 61

G

Gestures 39, 55
Glances 45, 47, 53, 55, 57, 58, 60, 62

H

Handling 187
Handoff 39, 65, 66
Handwashing 12, 18, 168
Haptics 43, 44
Health .. 19, 73, 153, 154, 161, 171
Hearing 19, 74
Heart Rate 152

I

iCloud 62
Installing / Removing Apps 67, 69, 105, 187
iTunes 64, 174, 202, 226
iTunes Match 202

M

Mail 127, 128, 129
Maps 19, 53, 136, 139, 225
Memoji 18, 83, 102, 116, 117, 119, 120, 121, 122, 123, 126
Messages ... 19, 121, 124, 127, 224
Music . 12, 142, 202, 203, 205, 209, 212, 215, 216, 219, 221, 225

N

Noise 71, 72
Notifications 51, 57, 72

O

Orientation 41

P

Pairing 33
Phone Calls 131
Photo Album 140
Photo Albums 142
Power Reserve 46, 47, 49

R

Reminders 12, 135
Remote Control 174
Rower 148

S

Side Button 63
Siri .. 12, 19, 28, 61, 62, 96, 97, 116, 130, 131, 134, 135, 142, 143, 166, 220, 225
Software Updates .31, 32, 189
SOS 12, 23, 36, 71
Sound 129, 221
Sounds 43, 44
Status Icon 51
Status Icons 51
Stocks 143, 226
Stopwatch 164, 226
Storage 140, 218

T

Text Messages ...19, 121, 124, 127, 224
Text Size 43
Trash 129
TV 117, 148, 151, 174, 175, 203, 226

V

Viewfinder 141
VoiceOver 186
VoiceOVer 186

W

Walkie-Talkie 54, 117, 175, 176
Watch Face 17, 76, 79, 102, 104, 105, 107, 120
Weather........... 143, 144, 226
WiFi.. 25, 28, 52, 53, 174, 183, 226

Workout App............... 54, 147

Y

Yoga 148

Z

Zooming 61

ABOUT THE AUTHOR

Scott La Counte is a librarian and writer. His first book, *Quiet, Please: Dispatches from a Public Librarian* (Da Capo 2008) was the editor's choice for the Chicago Tribune and a Discovery title for the Los Angeles Times; in 2011, he published the YA book The N00b Warriors, which became a #1 Amazon bestseller; his most recent book is *#OrganicJesus: Finding Your Way to an Unprocessed, GMO-Free Christianity* (Kregel 2016).

He has written dozens of best-selling how-to guides on tech products.

You can connect with him at ScottDouglas.org.

Made in the USA
Las Vegas, NV
14 May 2022